STARTING AN ONLINE BUSINESS FROM ZERO

A PROVEN GUIDE TO BREAK FREE FROM 9-5, SURF
THE DIGITAL WAVE AND WIN CUSTOMER TRUST

THE CONSULTING CLUB

CONTENTS

INTRODUCTION

> *"When everything seems to be going against you, remember that the airplane takes off against the wind, not with it."*

— **HENRY FORD**

We know from experience how it feels when you work in a job for someone else. We struggled with the 9–5 routine and frequently felt bored and frustrated by our jobs. We were often pushed to go the extra mile, with the promise of a reward of a promotion that seemed very hard to reach. We didn't feel we could use our creativity and imagination, or at times even think for ourselves and make decisions without it being run by managers, committees, and panels. We've had other jobs in the past where the office politics have been exhausting and relentless. We've been fortunate to have some charismatic bosses, but because we've experienced the good, we can also tell when we've had bad bosses who were authoritative and micro-managers.

I think the tipping point for us was having people in power higher up in the organization who treat others disrespectfully (we've sadly experienced bullies, and we've experienced people who take the credit for our hard work!). We've also had people who have expected us to work all hours at very short notice for ultimately little reward. While taking pride in your work is important, so is self-respect and not being a pushover! Without wanting to sound ungrateful, conceited, or arrogant, we often know we have better qualifications, skills, and experience than those we were working for! So, we figured if they could run a business, we certainly could too!

When you work for yourself, you are your own boss, you have control of what is going on, you are the one deciding the direction of the business, you choose your own hours, you can be creative, and any profit you make is yours!

Do you want to start an online business from zero? It can be challenging and a little daunting to do this completely alone. This book is here to be both a guide to starting a new online business and a companion and confidant for you on your journey to becoming a successful entrepreneur. This book will provide useful information and motivate and encourage you in the same way a knowledgeable, friendly mentor would.

It's perfectly natural and normal to have a few fears; Andrew Morgan of Marknology says, "Entrepreneurs are scared of all types of stuff and deal with more fear than most people. They fear not trying at all."[1] So, it is normal to have fears, but you need to push through these to create the life you want to achieve.

Many people who have transitioned to being an entrepreneur and running their own businesses have had their reasons for doing so. Laura Conaway thought women were underrepresented in tech, so she started InnovateHer KC to support women leaders. The Perkins Brothers build houses, but instead of subcontracting, they take a hands-on approach to ensure quality; they also have 300,000 subscribers on YouTube. Joel Johnson invented Mixtape, the Game in a card and app version and has sold over 100,000 decks. Needing money to pay their mortgage, Hernan Sias and his brother started a PC repair service called Business Bros.[2] These are just some examples of normal people *-like you, and like us-* that decided to take action and got rewarded with a successful business. Like them, there's millions of people that manage to create online businesses around the world, so why would it be different for you?

WHY SHOULD I READ THIS BOOK?

If any of the situations below apply to you, reading this book could help you:

- You currently **work full-time and want an exit strategy** to transition to running your own online business. You dislike working for someone 9–5 indefinitely in a job you don't love! Perhaps it frustrates you that your work is building your boss's business/improving their lifestyle, but ultimately not yours. Do you get the Sunday night blues when you're about to head back to work for another week? Do you feel restricted by your job? Are you tired of petty office politics and power struggles?

- You're **in between jobs and want to start your own online business**. Working for others who seem to take credit for your ideas or constrain your creativity can be tough when you're entrepreneurially minded. The routine of a workplace may not fit with your lifestyle. Being reliant on others for work may not suit you. It's nice to be responsible for making the decisions and be free to do things your way.

- You have already **recently started your own online business** but would like it to generate more income.

- You spend time **thinking about "making it" and becoming wealthy**. You want to make and invest money. You want to improve your lifestyle now and in the future (so you have a comfortable retirement). You may be keen to try new money-making ideas and enjoy listening to entrepreneurship or real estate podcasts or reading books on leadership and business. You may have seen that other people (some much younger than you -*even high school kids*-) have managed to make money with an online business, and you think it should be possible for you too, to create a profitable online business!

- **You want to build an online business based on something you have a passion for or have loved for a long time**, but you lack the confidence to do this. Perhaps you have self-doubt or self-limiting beliefs about your ability to build a business from scratch. You may feel that you lack the skillset you require.

- You may want to run your own online business to have it work for you even when you're not working. When a business works for you (instead of you working for a business), it **frees up more time for you to pursue activities** like traveling, reading, learning new skills, spending time with your loved ones, etc.

- **You can't find relevant, up-to-date, and easy-to-understand guidance.** Many business books are hefty and quite academic. Their ideas are outdated for online businesses or, at best, hard to relate to. This book will provide easy step-by-step instructions to guide you without swamping you in excessive nitty-gritty details. This book will boost your confidence so you know you can make your online business successful.

- Or maybe, **you want to emulate famous entrepreneurs** like those in the section below who started small and had crazy success.

Gary Vee, the Belarusian-American entrepreneur who diversified his income streams, is a five-time New York Times best-selling author, speaker, and Internet personality (who created VaynerX, VeeFriends, Wine Library TV, Resy, and Empathy Wines). One of Gary Vee's key quotes is: "Legacy is greater than currency." Gary Vee makes over $200 million a year from a marketing agency for a full spectrum of big companies (VaynerMedia) and for smaller Fortune 500 companies where he claims to "help ambitious businesses outgrow us" (The Sasha

Group). He also offers consultancy to professional athletes in the NFL, MLB, UFC, and eSports (VaynerSports).[3]

Perhaps **Jeff Bezos** is your hero, the chairman and the founder of Amazon. He initially created the e-commerce giant in 1994 from his garage in Seattle to sell books, then later a wide variety of products, including electronics and hardware. Amazon is the largest retailer on the World Wide Web. Amazon is open 24 hours daily and offers discounts, personalized recommendations, etc. Bezos owns *The Washington Post* and Blue Origin (aerospace rocket company). A key quote from Bezos is: "I didn't think I'd regret trying and failing. And I suspected I would always be haunted by a decision not to try at all."[4] Bezos controls the Whole Foods grocery chain and offers cloud computing and streaming services. He had a revenue with Amazon of $470 billion in 2021.[5]

Maybe **Steve Jobs** is whom you are looking up to; he created Apple Inc. and NeXT, Inc. He and Stephen Wozniak created a computer logic board in the Jobs' family garage, which they called the Apple I, which helped make the PC available to a broad audience. Jobs also acquired a controlling interest in Pixar and turned this into a major animation studio.[6] Jobs later created the iMac, iBook, iTunes, iPod (a portable MP3 player), iPhones, and iPod Touch. One of Jobs' quotes is: "We have an environment where excellence is expected . . . My best contribution is not settling for anything for the really good stuff, in all the details." Like Gary Vee's quote about legacy, Steve Jobs says too: "When I started, I was 20 or 21, and my role models were the semiconductor guys like Robert Noyce and Andy Grove of Intel, and of course Bill Hewlett and David Packard.

They were out not so much to make money as to change the world and to build companies that could keep growing and changing. They left incredible legacies . . . It's like when you're a parent . . . what's truly rewarding is living with your child and helping him grow up." [7] Steve Jobs also talks a lot about getting things right the first time, rather than fixing things and not putting out products until you feel they're right. It was important for him to build the best thing they could build.[8]

Or maybe it is **Oprah Winfrey** in whose footsteps you are striving to follow. Oprah is an American television personality, actress, and entrepreneur. Oprah has magazines called *O, The Oprah Magazine,* and *O At Home.* Oprah started as a news anchor, working on many shows as a reporter and then cohost before hosting talk shows. After acting in movies, she created her own television production company, Harpo Films. She started an on-air book club. She launched a cable television network for women. She has also engaged in many philanthropic activities, such as opening a school in South Africa, speaking against child abuse, and speaking about racial and gender equality.[9]

If the answer is 'Yes' to any of the above reasons, then keep reading, and this book will surely help you.

WHAT WILL I LEARN FROM THE BOOK?

- Seven steps to plan and build an online business from scratch.

- How to get a business up and running and feel prepared to start your online business.
- Methods for how to find a viable niche for an online business.
- How to price goods/services appropriately.
- How to create a compelling digital brand that resonates with customers.
- How to win the trust of customers and create repeat purchasers.

WHO ARE THE AUTHORS?

We are The Consulting Club. We are entrepreneurs and consultants whose work helps readers or club members establish and maintain successful consulting or online businesses. Some members do this part-time in addition to their existing employment; others run their own businesses. Our books provide readers with practical tools, best practices, and targeted advice gained from over 10+ years of firsthand experience.

We love to travel and have lived in nine different countries, spending much time in France, Spain, and Germany. Living and working in different countries has enabled us to address the needs and issues of customers from other cultures.

WHY HAVE WE WRITTEN THIS BOOK?

1. Our businesses have seen huge successes year after year. We realized we had the expertise to help other entrepreneurs, so we set up The Consulting Club.

We've worked in consulting for over ten years and helped startups in the healthcare and tech industries. Our experience as entrepreneurs and the insight gained from clients in other industries have given us a good understanding of what it takes to launch a successful online business.

2. We're passionate about helping others break free from the 9–5 culture through entrepreneurship. We know from our own experience that entrepreneurship can give you financial freedom. We have experience in turning failures into strengths and are committed to using our experiences to help others. Whatever you're truly passionate about is the key to your wealth and career. When starting, we benefited from the experience of other consultants and entrepreneurs. We feel it is time to return and share this knowledge with the entrepreneurial community.

3. We believe that when people are empowered to master their potential and hone their skills in helping others grow, we can improve the world.

WHAT ARE THE BENEFITS/RESULTS/OUTCOMES OF READING THIS BOOK?

1. You'll no longer dread going to work on a Monday
2. You won't have to conform to the same 9–5 grind that other people are shackled to

There's an Internet meme by Ellen Goodman, which I'm sure resonates with many:

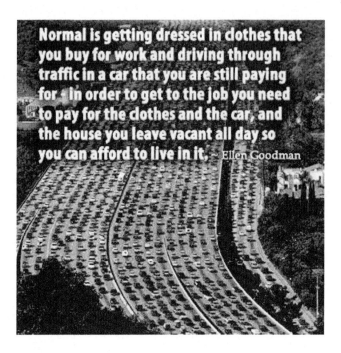

3. You'll be free to create your own schedule and choose what you want to work on.

4. You can become self-sufficient.

5. You can develop self-confidence and recognize your ability to achieve whatever you want.

1

DEVELOPING AN ENTREPRENEURIAL MINDSET

This chapter discusses what it takes to have an entrepreneurial mindset and why it's necessary for success.

There are forty-one million solopreneurs in the US alone, a steadily rising figure. The global pandemic brought a startup boom as many laid-off people started their own businesses. Also, technological changes have created an industry structure that means smaller firms can have a bigger piece of the market.

It is motivating to see that 20% of full-time independents earn a six-figure income and report to be very satisfied with their careers. They love the freedom they have to work in the way they want to, and 82% said they were happier working on their own. It is interesting to see that 53% of entrepreneurs felt more secure working independently than being employed. So after reading these facts, it comes as no surprise that in 2021 one in three Americans said to have a side hustle.[1] You might be wondering . . . which kind of side hustle? Well, we got you! In this book we will focus on online businesses specifically.

Online businesses surprisingly only contribute to 14% of all retail sales. However, e-commerce giants like Amazon have begun to chip away the market share of traditional retailers like Wal-Mart. So, even Wal-Mart has begun ramping up its online platform, which signals the growing preference for online business models.

But only some people who want to be entrepreneurs are cut out to start and run their own businesses. There are 4.5 million online businesses that start each year, but many of them will fail. Online business failure statistics show that 90% of e-commerce startups fail within 120 days of operation due to poor marketing and no search engine visibility.[2] Over a third of owners think this is because they can't compete with top brands, and 31% say it is because of a lack of funds. Almost 90% of e-commerce businesses fail because of poor product content, i.e., grainy photos or poorly written copy. This is why once you decide to venture yourself in the world of online businesses, it is wise to seek some guidance. We will provide you the basic steps you need to follow to avoid the pitfalls, but you'll also have to work hard and give it your all!

<u>The 4 top reasons why businesses fail include:</u>

1. Website issues

Sometimes it is because of too many issues and complications in the checkout process. You would be surprised to see how many businesses have poor websites that make it hard for the customer to even make a purchase. Other common issues are not aligning pricing and ads or not having a clear return policy. Some people ignore the importance of mobile UX (User Experience). Others don't have a robust backend. If there is poor site navigation, annoying pop-ups, required registration, and no customer service available (have someone who can answer questions), these are all things that will discourage users.

2. Business planning issues

One major reason is not having the cash flow to fund the business. Or having prepared cashflow for only a short period of time. Other reasons for failure include poor planning and testing of products or working in saturated niches.

3. Poor marketing

You could have the best product/service in the world, but if you do not have a good marketing strategy no one will notice your product (or your potential reach will be way smaller). Some owners also disregard SEO (Search Engine Optimization) and do not optimize their marketing strategy to appear in the relevant channels. As a basic part of your marketing strategy, you should have a good website, brand name, and business cards ready.[3]

4. Not having an entrepreneurial mindset

Some businesses fail because people give up too easily (try 3–5 products before quitting). We will discuss what an entrepreneurial mindset means in the next section.

WHAT IS AN ENTREPRENEURIAL MINDSET?

With an entrepreneurial mindset, you can adapt to any environment and build a successful business with the resources available to you. These skills transcend the realm of business and are about a person's self-reliance and problem-solving skills to solve the problems of customers, partners, employers, and the whole company.[4] As an entrepreneur, you must recognize opportunities and be innovative in facing challenges.

The top 5 traits you should have as an entrepreneur are:

1. A critical thinker with problem-solving skills.
2. Flexible and adaptable.
3. A great communicator, able to collaborate.
4. Comfortable with risk.
5. Self-reliant, able to work using your initiative oriented toward the future.[5]

Some debate whether an entrepreneur is born with those characteristics or can develop them over time. Research has shown that if you're raised in an entrepreneurial home, this can improve your chances of being an entrepreneur, but there are other important factors too. If parents raise children to work hard, answer questions, and let the child have self-determination, this will boost entrepreneurial instincts.[6]

An entrepreneurial mindset will help you develop skills that spill over into other parts of your life, such as minimizing the importance of failure and rejection. It will boost creative thinking and give you soft skills such as social interaction, communication, and listening. Planning and foreseeing potential problems will give you greater organizational skills and lead to a less stressful life.

When you have an entrepreneurial mindset, you'll think outside the box and know that there's often more than one solution to problems.[7]

THE 13 KEY CHARACTERISTICS OF SUCCESSFUL ENTREPRENEURS

1. Independence

As an entrepreneur, you will follow your instinct and do your own thing. There is an important quote from Steve Jobs: "Don't let the noise of other's opinions drown out your inner voice." You must be comfortable to trust your gut.

2. Responsibility and self-accountability

You need to take full responsibility as an entrepreneur, not blame others, and be the one to improve things.

3. Abundance mindset

Believe that you can improve your career by becoming an entrepreneur, making money with a successful business, and creating opportunities to live the life you want in the future.

4. Goal-oriented

Don't have wishes and dreams. Have goals and plans, and make the goals SMART (Specific, Measurable, Attainable, Relevant, and Time Sensitive). SMART goals help make the goal successful; this method gives you a sense of direction and helps you organize and reach your goals.

5. Not afraid of failure

Don't fear failure but look at it as a learning opportunity. Thomas Edison's famous quote is apt: "I have not failed. I've just found 10,000 ways that won't work." If you fail at something *that* has failed, you must try again. It doesn't mean *you're* a failure!

6. Growth-oriented and constantly learning

You can have a fixed mindset or a growth mindset. You don't believe you can change much if you have a fixed mindset. Most entrepreneurs have a growth mindset and think they can grow, learn, and develop new skills. When you constantly strive to self-educate and learn, this will help you succeed; Jim Rohn states: "Formal education will make you a living; self-education will make you a fortune." As an entrepreneur, there's a lot you'll have to learn, including talent management, issue resolution, and perhaps software skills to run your business better.[8] It would be best if you had flexibility as you may need to wear different hats and be on a constant learning curve.

7. Forward-thinking/long-term perspective

Whatever your actions today, think about how that will impact your future self. So, you could sit watching a TV program, but in most cases, that doesn't develop you for the future. So, instead of watching TV, you could take an online course. Instead of playing a computer game, an entrepreneur may tweak their sales funnel. Instead of spending considerable time on social media, an entrepreneur may listen to a motivational podcast or read a business book. The fact that you're reading this book shows you're forward-thinking and have a long-term perspective. A quote by billionaire investor Warren Buffet: "Someone is sitting in the shade today because someone planted a tree a long time ago." Most entrepreneurs have a goal in mind, and they reverse engineer that goal and work backwards from it to determine the steps they need to take.

8. Self-awareness

When you're self-aware, you acknowledge your strengths and weaknesses, which can help you know what you're good at. Play to your strengths and improve your weaknesses.

9. Collaborative

There are things you won't be as adept at doing, so you can call upon other people's expertise. It can also be good to have people bounce ideas off, keep them fresh, and move forward.

10. Comfortable with being uncomfortable

You need to be brave and have the courage to be an entrepreneur. Believe in yourself and your business even when times are tough. Indeed, you should even practice moving into uncomfortable situations. Jia Jang, an entrepreneur and keynote speaker, realized he feared rejection. I don't think any of us love it. But Jia faced his fears head-on and deliberately spent one hundred days getting rejected on purpose to overcome his fear. There are no 'safety nets.' There's no one above you to turn to if you have challenges (like in employment, where you may have a supervisor or boss). You don't have clear work boundaries or a steady paycheck. You have to learn to be okay with the risk. Suppose you have a team; you still need to pay them, even if you don't make any money in a week.[9] Entrepreneurs face rejection, risk, failure, embarrassment, anxiety, criticism, tears, and doubt.[10] If you're anything like us, even when you achieve success, there will be some days when you wonder if you've done the right thing, but then there are many other days when you're certain this is what you're meant to do!

11. Problem-solving skills

Entrepreneurs try to find solutions to problems that make people's lives better. For example, McDonald's provides food to people that want something cheap, fast and tasty.

Amazon Prime allows you to shop 24 hours a day and get your items delivered to your home the next day, providing a solution of convenience for people who don't want to go out to physical shops.

The co-founder of Airbnb, Brian Chesky, said, "If we tried to think of a good idea, we wouldn't have been able to . . . You just have to find the solution for a problem in your own life."

12. Action-oriented/decisive

Many people (and I'm sure you know a few) want to be entrepreneurs. Still, they spend most of their time reading books, watching videos, and making plans, but they never actually do the entrepreneurial work. At the same time, true entrepreneurs get on with it. They act. Walt Disney said "The way to get started is to quit talking and begin doing." As an entrepreneur, you'll also need to make swift decisions, sometimes without having all the information. As an entrepreneur, you will have the drive; you HAVE to because it's *you* running your business!

13. Resourcefulness

Specially when you start, you must maximize your available resources and don't wait until you have the perfect amount of money or knowledge. An obstacle we encountered at the beginning was that we did not have the budget to hire a developer to create a landing page, so we had to get hands on and learn with YouTube videos how to do it. It was not perfect, but it increased our knowledge and got our business started.

7 EFFECTIVE WAYS TO DEVELOP AN ENTREPRENEURIAL MINDSET TO MAXIMIZE YOUR LONG-TERM SURVIVAL

An entrepreneurial mindset is thinking in ways that help you achieve your goals of creating, developing, and running your own business. You will embrace challenges, mistakes, and failures and see them as opportunities to gain new skills that will help you succeed. You do not require an MBA to have an entrepreneurial mindset (although education is always good). An entrepreneurial mindset makes you perform at high levels and achieve more, allowing you to develop your business ideas fully.[11] Below are seven ways to help you develop an entrepreneurial mindset and survive as a business:

1. Commit to your passion

Do what you love, enjoy, and are passionate about. This way, it won't seem like a chore, and your enthusiasm and commitment to this will shine through. Be your coach and cheerleader in your ability to be successful with your business. Take your business seriously and be responsible. You can commit to your passion by setting goals and making daily progress; you will achieve what you want when you keep chipping away each day! It can be a good idea to write down your goals, as people who write them down are 42% more likely to achieve them than people who don't.[12] Keep on persevering, even when times are tough.

2. Embrace experimentation and new ideas

Try new things with your business. It could be new products, new pricing, or gaining feedback from advisers. If something isn't working for you, be prepared to change or abandon it. New ideas and new knowledge are coming out all the time. Open up to this and keep on learning. Well-known entrepreneurs such as Warren Buffett, Elon Musk, Mark Zuckerberg, and Bill Gates make time to read daily.

3. Understand your strengths and weaknesses

Gaining consumer feedback is important and a good way to help understand your strengths and weaknesses. You can use surveys, social media, studies, focus groups, complaints, etc.

4. Protect your time

Time is money. Be wise when choosing which projects you are working on. Make sure that your daily actions are bringing you closer to your goal and do not get distracted along the way by other things that might consume your precious time.

5. Always look for networking opportunities

It's good to spend time with other entrepreneurs. The people you surround yourself with can have quite an impact on you, so if you have people around who are energized, inspired, and optimistic, this will make you feel that way too. Also, they may have been in your shoes recently and can pass on valuable advice. Harvard Business School classmates Jenny Fleiss and Jenn Hyman met each week for lunch to brainstorm ideas, and their business of renting out designer dresses has been a huge success, with a $1B valuation.[13] Exchanging ideas with others is crucial and could lead to you meeting a future business partner![14]

6. Never stop learning

Keep abreast of changes in the digital world, the developments, and trends, such as Google SERPs and user search behavior (during the pandemic, users shifted from mobile to desktop devices due to being at home). Amazon affiliate commission changed; digital marketing and SEO strategies need constant tweaking/changing. Google will regularly update algorithms. Display ads have greater importance in keeping revenue flowing into businesses. It's important to keep creating the best possible quality content. Keep up to date with consumer tastes and buying preferences.

7. Digitally specific

Focus on what works in your business instead of experimenting

Track metrics to see what is working and do more of that!

Steer clear of shiny objects

Technology progresses rapidly, and people fear being left behind. But you don't have to do everything and be everywhere at once. Look at what works for your business and learn from past mistakes. Essentially, if you purchase shiny objects but don't know how to use them well, they won't give you a competitive edge. Consider your audience, business gaps, whether the technology will help close the business gaps, and whether you can sustain the technology long term.[15]

Think about diversifying the way you do business with different channels

Explore multiple channels to bring your business the best results. Don't just rely on a single channel. Consumers have many ways of researching products, interacting with brands, and ways to make purchases, and they will move through multiple channels before deciding to buy.[16]

Find as many ways as possible to generate income from one business

This is also known as 'income stacking.' It's a way to build multiple streams of income for your business. There will be many options, and you need to determine what will give you the best return on investment. You could consider YouTube advertising campaigns or training and developing your sales team.

Chapter Checklist:

1. Identify three entrepreneurial characteristics that you most associate with.
2. Find three characteristics that you want to build for yourself.
3. Pick one activity you can use to help you practice improving at least one of those characteristics you want to develop.

This chapter has covered what an entrepreneurial mindset is and why it's needed to be successful. Some key takeaways are that the chapter has shown that entrepreneurs enjoy their work, feel free, experience better health, and have job security.

Many qualities make an entrepreneurial mindset. An entrepreneur should be adaptable, self-reliant, able to solve problems/come up with solutions, and be comfortable with risk. The good news is that these skills can all be learned!

One key aspect is that entrepreneurs should take action and be decisive! This part of the mindset can be applied to the next chapter about finding trends to develop a viable business idea! There's no time to act and start your entrepreneurial journey like the present!

2

THE TREND IS YOUR FRIEND

In this chapter we will first look at what's the best way to research trends so that you can generate a business idea and then, we will explain some strategies that you can use to promote your business and attract customers.

The Internet has changed our lives forever. Most people use the Internet to shop online, communicate with friends and family, and for entertainment. This means you have access to a huge audience of potential customers who could be interested in your products or services. You are no longer limited to your geographical area to make money and that's definitely great news!

THE TOP DIGITAL BUSINESS TRENDS TO WATCH

Over the past ten years, several digital business trends have changed how online businesses interact with customers. We will discuss some of the top trends below because, depending on your business, some of these could help you succeed. It's not necessary to be at the top of every trend. Still, it is very important for a business owner to stay updated with the market trends to have control of what is happening.

We are going to show you the trends that we believe are going to be relevant in the next year. You should watch them and understand them to see how they can best serve you. Maybe you can even come with a business idea by reading about them!

- **Voice Search Optimization (VSO)**

Suppose you have a digital business and still need to start using VSO. In that case, you're missing out on people finding your website through voice searches like Microsoft Cortana, Amazon Alexa, or Google Assistant. You're missing out on a great opportunity as 58.6% of US consumers use VSO. Voice searches currently comprise 20% of mobile searches, which is expected to increase with time. It is predicted that 75% of US households will own a smart speaker by 2025.[1]

- **Chatbots and Conversational AI**

Forty-two percent of consumers use conversational AI and chatbots when making purchases, often to ask FAQs about the product. However, many small business owners don't use this technology (perhaps due to cost), but the benefits of doing so include personalization and FAQs dealt with swiftly.[2] Chatbots can answer customers' basic questions 24 hours a day and give a 'controlled message.' They can behave in a very real way, and sometimes customers don't know they're not real. What is good about them is that they collect data, which you can use to improve the customer experience. The trend is to use AI to make bots form sentences that convey emotion; customers will feel that brands care about them. There may also be a trend of personal shopping assistant bots, using previous data to help anticipate products you will like.[3]

- **Data Analytics**

Data is how we can differentiate a successful business from another, and it is what makes a business sustainable in times of crisis, such as a recession. Customer data can be used to differentiate businesses, understand customers and campaigns, optimize them, and use it to build the brand.[4] Marketers need to learn how to use the data they collect. They may have information from customers about purchase behavior, favorite products, and the best ways to reach them. You could use this data for more personalized adverts or targeted coupons/deals. There are likely to be trends in edge computing for faster analysis and machine learning-driven solutions.

- **User Experience (UX)**

Customers expect to be able to navigate through the online experience smoothly. The site should be engaging, user-friendly, convenient, interactive, experiential, and personalized. Sites should work quickly and be visually stable, mobile-friendly, and safe.

- **The Metaverse**

This is a blend of virtual reality (VR), augmented reality (AR), and artificial intelligence (AI). This can include interactive ads allowing people to "feel" experiences and "gamevertising," where marketers/brands use games for advertising products. An example of this is NASCAR's ad on the gaming platform Roblox.[5] This trend is because customers want experiences to be as realistic, interactive, and immersive as possible. Anything encouraging customers to feel emotions will help develop a better relationship with the brand.

- **SEO and Keywords**

SEO and keywords continue to be important. Google's page experience algorithm assesses loading speed, interactivity, visual stability, and HTTPS security. There is also Google's Mobile-First Indexing (MFI) that ranks mobile-friendly websites. If you have authoritative content on your site, this is beneficial. So do not underestimate the power of having an up-to-date blog with posts about actual trends in your niche.

- **No Cookies for You**

People dislike data collection and feel it invades their privacy. Google will roll out a cookie phase-out. Because cookies collect emails, advertisers and marketers will want to think about cookie alternatives. This is a trend because it will impact all sites that currently use cookies, and they will need to use something different.

- **Social Media Marketing (SMM)**

Key to social media are things like video, Instagram, live streaming, and podcasts. Facebook and LinkedIn remain popular. Communicate with customers and tell brand stories. This is a trend because people spend a lot of time on social media each day, and people want to know how to reach a market in places where they naturally spend time.

- **Augmented Reality**

Retail brands can use avatars that buyers create to try on clothes, sit on chairs, live in geographical areas, etc. Thirty-five percent of people have said that they would shop online more if they could virtually try on a product before buying it.[6] This is a trend because it helps make online shopping more immersive and realistic and increases customers.

- **New Payment Methods**

Businesses may use DeFi (decentralized finance), such as blockchain, cryptocurrency, and non-fungible tokens (NFTs). As a curious fact, we have recently seen retail condos in Manhattan that have put on sale and you can buy them with Bitcoin![7] This is just an example of how things are changing and a reminder that you should never stop investigating new trends, you don't want to miss on sales because you do not support a certain type of payment!

- **Customer Subscriptions**

Subscription models are changing the digital space. They allow companies to plan for inventory and sales that are already locked in. There will be a trend for more companies to offer subscription or monthly payment options for larger purchases because it helps people manage their finances in smaller installments.

TRACKING CONSUMER TRENDS WITH GOOGLE

Why should you invest time in researching trends? Easy, it's the only way you have to stay ahead of what your customer is going to ask from you in the next months. One tool we really like is Google Trends; we use it because it tells you how popular a search term is in Google (i.e., how many people are searching for it). The benefits of this are that it will allow you as a business to prepare for shifts in customer interest and be aware of what people are or are not searching for. The searches change over time, by season, and by geographical location. It can let you know how your niche product is trending. You can also use it to edge out competitors by monitoring their positions.

Below is a list of our favorite ways to track consumer trends via Google:

- **Find Relevant Product Categories in Related Topics**

You can compare two search topics to see which one is more popular with users. You add a topic, click '+ Compare,' and add your second topic. This gives you a quick idea of which product is in greater demand/more popular and may increase your sales. It helps you to know what you should promote. This can be useful for seasonal holidays, such as Mother's Day, and a florist wanting to know whether 'flower delivery' or 'gift baskets' are more popular. It will generate a graph where you can see both trends. You can adjust the dates of your search to see trends over time.[8]

Practical example: Type in your search word that sells well, then scroll down to the bottom, and you'll find 'Related topics.' For example, if you sold 'fake eyelashes,' the related topics could be eyelash extensions, artificial hair integrations, adhesives, nails, etc. [9] You could make a Google Trends comparison to see your competitors' performance by putting in 2–5 different brands.

- **Using Google Trends for Keyword Research**

If you're searching for a term in Google, Google Trends will allow you to see whether it's a rising or declining trend. It's worth expanding the range from 2004 to the present, rather than the default 'past 12 months' to have a really good view of whether it's increasing or declining and you'll also get an overview of the seasonal trends by doing this. If the graph it produces goes up and up over time, you can see that there has been skyrocketing growth; you'll also see if there are any dips in searches for it.[10] If a graph looks pretty stable up and down, you'll determine that the niche is fairly stable. If you see any dips, it just means that you may have a lower volume of website traffic at those times of the year. If something is a passing 'fad,' you'll see there were no searches before a certain date, a sharp spike of interest, then it'll drop back down to virtually zero (this could be seen in 2017 with the craze for 'fidget spinners').[11] Using Google Trends can help you find the best keywords, considering regional differences in phrase preference. You can test out related phrases, i.e., soda vs. pop vs. coke.

If you want to find out which keywords you should use in your sites, once you've searched for a trend, you can look at 'Related queries,' which is on the right side of 'Related topics,' which will bring up keywords. For example, if you were selling clothes, you may see certain colors stand out, and you could include them in your search terms.[12]

- **Finding Ideas for Content Marketing**

Google has a 'related topic' function; some topics it suggests might not always make sense for your business. But you could sometimes use the idea for a blog post. For example, if you had an online store selling beauty products, a related topic for 'fake eyelashes' is Kim Kardashian, although you can't sell Kim Kardashian as a product. Still, you can use the idea of her to blog (or comment on other social media channels) about her eyelashes. You can also use Google Trends for content freshness; this is where you remove outdated content, add fresh new details, and republish the content on your blog.

An example is if you owned a cycling store and had a blog article called 'How to Fix a Bike.' If you put those terms into Google Trends, you can see that people search for this in June and July each year, so you could ensure that your fresh content is targeted for the end of May; this would help grow website traffic. You can also look for 'trending searches,' which are the hottest current topic; they're real-time. Some will be celebrity news, but you'll see other trends like the Momo challenge of 2019. If you had a store that targeted the parents of young children, you could have an article about this on your blog or social media.[13] A current trend is Tesla; if you had a store that sold car accessories, you could have a blog about car manufacturers. By bringing audiences to your website, you increase the chance of sales.[14] It's important to educate the audience beyond just a purchase because this brings a bigger picture that can influence traffic and sales indirectly.

- **Looking for Niche Topics by Region**

Searching for a term in Google Trends will give you a heat map showing you where the term is most popular. If you hover over areas on the map, it will give a percentage of searches from that area. It will list the top cities and regions where people search for the term.[15]

You can break this down into states in America. If you see that your product is doing better in one state than another, you would be better to target that state if you promote it on Facebook or Google AdWords. You increase your chance of sales without wasting advertising money.

- **Google Trends YouTube**

On YouTube, if you look for particular videos relevant to your niche (e.g., fashion) and see what the keywords of the top video are (e.g., 'fashion trends 2019'), you could then put that keyword into Google Trends. If we do this exercise we will see that it's a keyword popular for January 2019. So any content that was created that year for these keywords ranked very well. If you look back at previous years to see patterns, you will see spikes in March and September, before summer and winter (seasonal peaks for this type of industry . . . depending on what industry you are aimed at, you may have peaks at different times of the year). If you have an email list, you could send an email to boost your video's popularity at these times.[16]

- **Google Trends Google Shopping**

You can use Google Trends to find the best time to create a Google Shopping ad. If you were a fashion retailer wanting to sell a black dress, you could look at Google Trends' Google Shopping feature to find the best months for your ad. You will see rises and dips and may decide to promote your dress between February to May and October to November.[17]

HOW TO VALIDATE TRENDS

It's important to validate trends because it can help you determine whether an idea is worth pursuing, help secure funding and resources, and bring a concept to reality. This section will give some suggestions on verifying the trends you've encountered in the previous section. We'll look at this in greater detail in the chapter on competitive market research, but in general, some good tips include:

- **Keeping up with industry research/reports**

Many free, reliable sources provide customer and market information, such as general business statistics, consumer statistics, demographics, etc. You can find these statistics from places like the Small Business Administration.[18]

- **Following industry influencers and publications**

You need to make sure you know the authority figures in your niche industry, follow, learn, and try to emulate them. Look at their blogs. Listen to their podcasts. Read their websites and reports. Follow them on LinkedIn and other social media. Meet them at networking events or conferences. Ninety percent of marketers think influencer marketing is effective. The average engagement rate with influencers is around 5.7%.[19] Influencer marketing channels include Instagram, YouTube, Facebook, blogs, and Twitter.

- **Conducting market research**

Market research is defined as the process of evaluating the feasibility of a new product or service through research conducted directly with potential consumers.[20]

Market research is important because you want to validate feedback, and to learn if there's a demand for your product/service, how many people may be interested in it, where your customers are based, whether they already have similar options to buy, and what customers would usually pay.

When you do market research, you'll look at consumer behavior and economic trends to inform your business. Market research reduces the chance of risk. You can consider population data on age, wealth, family, interests, or anything relevant to your selling.

You can conduct market research through surveys, questionnaires, focus groups, and in-depth interviews.

Competitive analysis is about identifying competition and assessing their market share, strengths, and weaknesses, your window of opportunity, whether your competitors will view your target market as important, any barriers, and any secondary competitors who may impact you.[21]

Chapter Checklist:

1. Choose three up-and-coming digital trends from the list above to monitor.
2. Use Google Trends to create a shortlist of three potential trends you can use as a basis for your business.
3. Write a list of at least three places where you can validate the trends and take a look at these.

3

HOW TO FIND YOUR NICHE

Have you spent hours thinking of a profitable niche you could try? Have you watched thousands of Youtube videos where a 19 year old teen explains how they became rich and they promise that you'll get the same results if you follow their method and get started in their 'bullet-proof' niche? Well, we also dig deep to find profitable niches where we could tap into. Sometimes it worked, sometimes it didn't. What we can assure you is that there is no bullet-proof method to find a profitable niche, but the things we are about to explain will certainly give you some tools to pave the way.

The Internet has become a powerful tool for businesses to reach customers. In fact, according to Statista, e-commerce sales increased from $1 trillion in 2010 to over $2 trillion in 2017; by 2021, it was over $5.2 trillion.[1] This means there are plenty of opportunities for entrepreneurs looking to start an online business.

WHAT IS A NICHE MARKET?

A niche market is simply a group of people that have the same interests or lifestyle and that could potentially be interested in your product. If you are listening to your niche needs and crafting a product that speaks to them you are providing high value. And when customers feel like they get high value from your offering, they will always buy again! When you have a niche, you are the 'go-to' brand for customers for a specific product type, and you are credible over other 'generalists' who sell other things, not in the niche area. You will have a unique value proposition and product line extensions. These things will make customers choose you.[2]

An example of this could be women's shoes, the larger market; there are many different makes and styles. Your niche could be that you specialize in vegan shoes, plus-sized shoes, or shoes specifically for nurses. You can have a cross-section of different audiences; for example, bikes are a large market, and mountain bikes are a niche, but an even more specialized niche could be mountain bikes for teens.[3]

Some niches are based on price (luxury, mid-price, discount); demographics (age, gender, income, education); quality (premium, handmade, economical); psychographics (values, interests, attitudes); or geographics (residents of a specific country, city, or neighborhood).[4]

A niche should solve a customer's problem and fulfill unmet needs![5]

HOW TO FIND YOUR NICHE

The niche you choose will determine how you market the product, its price, quality, and your position/branding.

Here are seven steps that will help you find a suitable niche:

Step 1: Think about what you're passionate about

List all the things, topics, and interests you know well and find fascinating. What do you enjoy doing in your free time? What do you enjoy learning about?[6] It could be something that you do as a hobby. It could be something people keep asking for your help with or tell you you're good at. It needs to be something you enjoy as you will put a lot of time and effort into working on it.

It has to be something that holds your interest now and long term; think about something you can still imagine being passionate about for 5+ years.[7] If it interests you, you can also discuss the niche area knowledgeably and add your personal experience/knowledge, which can be very valuable for people going through the same experience or having similar pain points. Niche audiences know their stuff. It's a good idea to put across content that establishes your credibility. Don't worry if the topics you list seem to have a limited appeal; there will likely be a like-minded audience who resonates with your niche. Once you have your list, think about solving problems that aren't currently being solved.[8]

Step 2: Consider your skills

Even if you think that you have no skills, we assure you that there is something where you have accumulated expertise. At this stage, most people (including ourselves) question themselves and think that they are not an expert in any area. Most of the time, this is related to the fact that we tend to underestimate our own capacities, but don't worry, we have found a formula that will help you to identify them.

First of all, sit and with the help of a pen and a paper write down all the things that you know how to do (if these are things that you also enjoy doing that's always extra points). If you do that exercise with consciousness, you will see that you come up with a long list of potential skills you can use in your niche. And don't panic, if you are interested in a niche where it seems like you don't have enough knowledge you can always take a course or read a book. The good thing about today's world is that most of the information is at a click of a distance, so don't get discouraged! A final suggestion for gaining a good indication of your skills is to ask for feedback from people, which could help you discover an area you're skilled at that could ultimately become a niche.[9]

Step 3: Link your expertise and passion to market demand

• Focus on the Problems

What you're looking for with your niche are gaps in the market. This is known as disruptive innovation, where innovation is a business's ability to create something new and better than before.[10] What problems aren't there currently solutions for? Then, using your expertise and skills, how could you resolve the problems? In the words of Bigweld from *Robots*: "See a need, fill a need." Take time to think about what you wish existed that doesn't currently. It's a customer's 'pain point' that you're trying to solve.[11]

Finding solutions to customers' issues can be very profitable. What are people willing to pay for? Notice what people are spending their money on. Your niche needs to serve your customers, and you need to prioritize them.

Jeff Bezos created the biggest online shopping marketplace. What was missing in the market? He bridged a gap that offered low prices at great convenience, so people used Amazon to make shopping easy! Similarly, Elon Musk found that money was difficult to transfer safely, and he bridged the gap by building PayPal, which made money transfers safe and easy.[12]

It can be a good idea to look at trends to find what customers are talking about, what matters to them, and what difficulties and issues they're having so that you can come up with a solution that solves it. See what is popular and whether you can make an even better version. Look at trends using Google

Trends (free) or other paid and free tools for trends, such as Hootsuite, BuzzSumo, Social Mention, and Feedly. You can also explore BuzzFeed and Hashtag Expert.[13] Pay attention to what is being discussed and understand what matters to your audience. If there is competition in a market, there is opportunity.[14] In researching a profitable niche, it's good to find the problem and issues the target audience has and evaluate the supply and demand to verify a potential.

- **Conduct Keyword Research**

Keyword research is important because it will help you see various trends and refine your niche. It is important to google your niche keywords, e.g., this could be 'cruelty-free makeup,' and see what options you could pick to go into. It will bring up 'vegan' options and 'not tested on animals.' You can explore different trends until you find an audience or demand.

Once you have found keywords that interest you and that you would like to explore further, it's useful to dig a bit deeper with some tools. We have used a tool called **Keywords Everywhere** (it's a browser extension) and it will display results for related keywords on the right of your screen everytime you search for a keyword, which is useful to create your offer. There are also paid research programs, including KWFinder, Ahrefs, SEMrush, and Moz. These range from $30 up to $999 per month.[15]

Take time to create content that shows you know a lot about your products, as this will help you with Google rankings.[16] An 'Exploding Topics' tool also allows entrepreneurs to find emerging trends before they take off.[17] You can also use a free keyword research tool like Ubersuggest, which will give you an overview of each phrase of search terms you put in. It will tell you if it's difficult to have as a niche and approximately how much it will cost per click.[18]

Step 4: Conduct competitive research to validate demand for products within the given niche(s)

With your competitors, you can look at what they're doing well and not so well to outperform them with your niche website.

- **Amazon Best-Seller Lists**

You can look at Amazon and search the best-seller list that relates to the niche you intend to sell. You can see what is selling well and think about ways to improve the product or better ways to market the product. Look at product reviews, see what customers like and dislike about the products, and how you can improve yours![19]

- **Affiliate Marketplace Best-Seller Lists**

Affiliate marketing is when a person (an affiliate) refers people to a company's products or services.[20] You don't have to use affiliate marketing to make money, but you can use the tools to determine whether a niche will be profitable. There are affiliate marketplaces like ShareASale, ClickBank, and CJ Affiliate that are free. You can search niche categories and look at the popularity of products in your niche market.

- **Drop Ship Best-Seller Lists**

Drop shipping is an order fulfillment method where a business doesn't keep the products it sells in stock; instead, the seller buys inventory as needed from a wholesaler or manufacturer to fulfill orders. Many people do drop shipping because less upfront capital is required, it's easy to start, there are low overheads, it can be run from anywhere with the Internet, there's a wide variety of products you could sell, and it's easy to scale.[21] Several drop ship marketplaces are free to join, like AliExpress and Oberlo. You can use the listing to research products in niche markets and explore whether starting a niche drop shipping business is worth it. You can search them by keyword, item name, and category, and filter sales over periods or by price.

- **Look for Online Communities**

People on the Internet organize themselves into communities based on shared interests, passions, and hobbies via Facebook groups, Slack, LinkedIn, Discord, Circle, Tribe, Hivebriet, Reddit threads, and others. People choose a platform for the community, develop a launch framework, identify stakeholders, set up the community, have a soft launch, and promote the community. It's important to have content in the community and market it. You can search the most visited Wikipedia pages under hobbies or the most active subreddits. You can look at Quora and other forums.[22] Listen to Instagram and Twitter hashtags to find opportunities that could be a niche.

- **Questions to Ask Potential Customers**

You may want to find out where they're located. Which social media sites do they use? What hobbies do they have? It would be good to know demographic data such as age and gender. Knowing the customer's goals, aspirations, careers, and the people they admire may be useful depending on your business.

Step 5: Narrow Down Your Niche

- **Look at niche markets vs. niche products/services**

One technique to find your niche is to start with a niche market and drill down further to find niche products. So, a niche could be 'conscious consumers' because six out of ten consumers are happy to change their shopping habits and to reduce environmental impact.

This opens up options for vegan, eco-friendly, and cruelty-free products that give a greener alternative. Examples of companies that do this include Bee's Wrap, which replaces cellophane wrap with products made from beeswax. Other options are reusable drinking straws and cruelty-free cosmetics. Another niche could be health and wellness; this lucrative market reached 1 trillion in 2020. Some sub-niches involve personal care, nutrition, and preventative and alternative medicines. There are many options in this niche of food, beverage, beauty, personal care, skin health, immunity, and digital products like ebooks and recipes. Other niche products under health and wellness include melatonin gummies, mushroom-infused coffee, massagers, kombucha brew kits, oil diffusers, etc.

- **Find a way to stand out in your niche**

Suppose you can find a competitive advantage that sellers on Amazon do not have. In that case, this will benefit your business as it's a USP (Unique Selling Point) that can differentiate your business from others. The examples below have narrowed the focus of their niche:

1. Cleaning services . . . for busy singles living in NY city apartments. So, in this example, the person stands out from other cleaning services by focusing on the niche of busy singles in NY city apartments. It's very specific regarding the demographic, the location, and the type of home they'll clean.
2. Painting classes . . . for retirees over sixty new to watercolor portraiture. In this example, the person isn't just offering painting classes to anyone. The very niche demographic is people who are retired, over sixty years old, and beginners to using watercolor paints, specifically to do portraits! Again, it's a very narrow specific niche of people, their career stage, age, level of competence with painting, the type of paints they'll use, and specifically what they'll paint with them. This is a very precise niche of the market.
3. Drone photography . . . for wedding photographers looking to add more services.[23] This is a specific niche because it's not suggesting the drone photographs are

aerial shots of someone's house or searching for lost pets; it's specifically targeted at weddings.

First, you could develop an Ideal Customer Profile (ICP) representing the perfect person you want to sell your product to. Knowing what customers you want to target allows you to tailor your niche market specifically to them.

MIND MAP

You could create a mind map with your niche in the center, then brainstorm for everything you can think of that stems from this. When you develop a mind map, from the general area of 'cruelty-free makeup,' you may come up with tangents of things for the face, cleansing, hair care products, and products for the body. This may allow you to refine your niche (or find related products to offer consumers).

- **Define your niche and its profitability**

There are two main concepts regarding your niche and its profitability:

1. Focusing on delivering value is important before thinking about how we can be profitable. You can follow the value selling methodology for this.
2. Analyze how profitable the niche could be in which you want to launch your business. (Give a high-level overview of the steps/tools required to work that out.)

It's important to over deliver on value. Have you heard of the concept of value selling? The value selling methodology focuses on how the product will provide value to the customer and not that much in the product per se. We discovered that ninety-two percent of buyers want to hear a value proposition early in the sales cycle.[24] It can be seen as a consultative approach to sales that conveys the value of a product or service along the way.[25] If you're selling something for $100, it's important to ensure that it delivers *more* than $100 worth of value.[26] Show the customer how your product will help him/her live a certain lifestyle, save time or make them feel good. If, for example, you were selling a short-handled screwdriver, it's good to let customers know it could save them 20 minutes a day, leading to a 5% increase in efficiency and lower costs.

Step 6: Find Out the Margins to Evaluate the Profitability of the Niche Market

- **Test your niche**

1. You should first create your audience by engaging with them before launch. You can do this in several ways: Kickstarter campaigns, crowdfunding, or gaining followers through email opt-in pages and social media campaigns.[27]
2. You should create a landing page or mockup store that promotes a free info product related to the niche. You can use a tool like Leadpages to do this and drive traffic to it with AdWords.[28]

3. You can survey your target market on guest posts, industry-related groups, Google Surveys, social media, etc. You can use canvas door-to-door or attend business fares to see other ideas and display yours.[29]

4. Take time to build a loyal customer base who will follow you to e-commerce when ready.[30] You can do this by providing content that customers find valuable and informative. You can create engaging social media content and respond to customers' comments. You can offer samples, promotions, and discounts. Any customers who praise your products try to engage online.

5. You could offer a product trial period or give out lead magnets (these are a free item or service that is given away to gather contact details); this could be educational content that helps the reader solve part of the problem you want to address with your business/service/product to target customers. While testing, you want to ensure this does not cost much money so that you don't incur a loss to the business before you begin.

- **Test with ads to be 100% sure it is profitable**

1. Are your adverts generating interest from consumers?
   The practical way to get traffic is through paid ads,
   PPC, AdWords, and referrals.[31] You should ideally invest
   a couple of hundred dollars in testing campaigns in
   AdWords and Facebook. This is a worthwhile
   investment to save you from losing money long term.[32]
   This is not just important to measure the profitability
   of the niche but also to refine your target group. Are
   your ads getting more traffic from teenagers or baby
   boomers? You can work out if there's enough demand
   for what you want to sell.

**Step 7: Validate Your Niche Ideas by Test Selling Specific
Products/Services Online**

1. You could start with a small batch of drop-shipping
   products and run a campaign to a targeted audience.
   Get feedback from the customers who have made their
   first purchases or send some out to influencers to gain
   their opinion. Get feedback early on; this can take time
   because you need to test, see the results, learn from this,
   and retry.

EXAMPLES OF SUCCESSFUL NICHE STRATEGIES

1. Sara Blakey couldn't find nice-looking, good quality, smooth
undergarments for women. So, she invented Spanx after
discovering that tights/pantyhose cut off at the foot would roll

up her legs but eliminated panty lines and made her body appear firmer.

She spent two years and approximately $8,300 of her own savings researching and developing the idea. She presented the idea to America's hosiery mills (mostly male-owned), who did not see the value in her idea. Two weeks later, one contacted her for support after his three daughters encouraged the idea. This evolved into a billionaire business niche.

2. The six co-founders of **Lush** could not find products that had not been tested on animals and were made from fresh organic products. This was their pain point, and after market research, they discovered other people would like non-animal-tested organic products too. They previously ran a mail-order business called 'Cosmetics to Go,' which collapsed due to over-trading and flooding, so they regrouped and created Lush. One founder introduced a supplier-specific boycott policy, which means Lush won't buy any ingredient from a supplier that tests any of its materials on animals for any purpose; this is unique in its field, different and distinct from the Humane Cosmetics Act standard. They didn't want their packaging to cost more than their product. Over the years, they keep trying to increase the natural ingredients in their products and reduce the synthetic ones and preservatives. Over the years, Lush has now grown to have 937 shops. There has been a 13.1% increase in 2021 sales.

3. **Kaioptics** have a niche market segment that solved the issue of poor-fitting glasses for Asian Americans. This is the area they specialize in, and most frames are under $100.[33]

4. SoulCycle was a studio solely with the niche of 45-minute indoor cycling to aid fitness. It has three co-founders, and its niche was that it transcended a workout from being a chore or necessity to something spiritual and physically empowering and emancipating. It was also very exclusive, with wealthy and famous clientele; people liked the desirability and exclusivity, where it was hard to get a spot to SoulCycle.

It had a stealthy location, and people heard about it via word of mouth. This meant the business struggled to scale because when it became more 'mainstream,' it lost its popularity, and that, along with the pandemic, brought demise to the business.[34]

5. Georgetown Cupcake, run by sisters Katherine Kallinis Berman and Sophie Kallinis LaMontagne, only sells cupcakes. They designed an affordable luxury brand and played on the niche of the childhood connection to baking at their grandmother's house. So, when customers visit, there is an emotional, nostalgic connection to childhood and family, which gives them good vibes.[35] Georgetown Cupcake focuses on one thing and does it really well. It has now grown to 7 locations, with 400 employees who sell and ship 25,000 cupcakes per day.

6. Nerd Fitness targets gamers and cosplayers who want to work out and be healthy.[36] It started as a blog and developed into a community with an online coaching program and a tracking app to track the fitness journey. They embrace the image of 'weirdos' and 'misfits' and encourage people to be themselves. Their niche differs from the stereotypical image of fitness. The founder started the business after their fitness struggle and frustration with diet and health supplements on the market. The founder deliberately shies away from ads or sponsorship so that information on the site isn't biased but based on experience.[37] The founder thought there weren't any companies helping people like him with desk jobs that love nerd culture to make healthier choices.

7. **Lume** is a brand with natural deodorant, producing amusing video adverts to gain customers. Their deodorant is for people who suffer from skin irritations from other deodorants. It's a niche market, but their videos have gained viral success.[38] The founder Shannon Klingman is an obstetrician and gynecologist; she realized that many gynecologists misdiagnose basic odors and itches as bacterial infections. She wanted to create a natural deodorant free from aluminum and baking soda; the first version of Lume was created in the kitchen. Her patent was filed twelve years before her deodorant formula was accepted. She received many rejections but kept on persevering.[39]

8. **Lefty's** is a store with products for left-handed people, 10–15% of the population. It's a required niche, though, and produces left-handed scissors and notebooks. They produce informational books for kids about telling the time, cutting with scissors, writing, and tying shoelaces. It was opened in 2008 by Margaret Majua and has stationery, cooking utensils, and clothing. There was previously a store in 1978 called the "Left Hand World" on Pier 39, but it closed due to family illness; for years, the management had calls from people wanting the store reopened. Lefty's opened there when the store became available and later moved to a larger space. They found that many left-handed products were discontinued

because the demand didn't support the production and marketing costs, so they manufactured their own products wherever possible.

Chapter Checklist:

1. Follow the steps above to find two niches you think are a good fit for you and your business (you can use the trends you identified from the previous chapter).
2. Spend some time reviewing the pros and cons of each niche.
3. Decide on one niche to pursue.
4. Identify candidate products or services in your niche, run tests to see the highest demand, and run tests to finalize the targeting.

This chapter has covered a niche market, a unique specialist segment (i.e., vegan shoes, as part of the larger women's shoes market).

It has explored ways to find your niche. You can consider your passion and skills, then connect your expertise and passion plus market demand. What problems or customer pain points need solving?

The next chapter will look at the power of brand positioning once you have your niche area of focus! Let's press on and make good progress.

4

THE POWER OF POSITIONING

This chapter discusses brand positioning, but more specifically, how you should position your business versus your competitors. If this still sounds a bit abstract don't worry, let's take a look to the example below to see how it works in real life:

Scratch Supply Co. is a US company that managed to create a strong community of people that enjoys making knitted products. Before growing dramatically thanks to COVID (and more people doing crafts at home), they thought a lot about how to position themselves and leverage their differences, so they focused on:

1. Understanding their core goal. Having a clear mission and building a strong community of repetitive purchasers and followers was important.

2. Analyzing and defining what was making them different from other field players (values on equity, respect for suppliers and their expertise, and inclusivity).
3. Exploring their ideal client profiles and how Scratch Supply Co. could play a role in their life.
4. Not only considering their clients but also their suppliers by helping them to become wholesalers.[1]

As you can see, the company did not focus on a single thing but different elements of the ecosystem of their business to have a strong positioning.

WHAT IS POSITIONING?

Brand Positioning

Brand positioning states how the company wants consumers to think about the brand. It must capture the essence of everything the brand does well and what it's about.[2] It's how your market sees you and will let potential consumers understand your business at a glance.[3] Positioning will add value to your store and put you ahead of the competition by making you stand out and differentiating your business. You can stand out in several ways: with a high-quality product, fantastic customer service, low prices, or because you care for the environment. But you need to state your brand position to your target audience, so they can decide whether you are the brand they want to purchase from.

If you have some marketing background or have studied marketing, you have probably heard about the 4 Ps of marketing by Philip Kotler (Product, Price, Place, and Promotion). He also mentions Positioning (and place)! By positioning with 'place,' he means ensuring that your company's offer and image stand out as being distinctive in the mind of your target market. You need to create a customer-focused value proposition and give your target market a good reason why they should buy from you. It's good if you can emotionally connect with customers. With your product, you need to answer who needs it and why? What does it do that competitors' products don't? The price must be what consumers are willing to pay, and you must cover the real and perceived value. The place is where the product should be available, whether in a store or online, and how it will be displayed. Placement is also about advertising the product to the right media so that customers know about it. A key example of outstanding placement was when the new BMW Z3 was shown in the 1995 Bond film *GoldenEye*, and even though the car hadn't been released at the time of the movie, BMW received nine hundred orders for the car! Promotion is about letting consumers know they need the product and that it is good value for money; it includes advertising, PR, and media strategy.[4]

Positioning Statement

When you're coming up with a positioning statement, you can think about the following:

1. What values does your ideal customer hold?
2. What are your values, and how do these connect to your company and the products you sell?
3. What are the key skills, areas of expertise, and things your company does well, and how can you make this visible?
4. What brands do you like, and how could people associate your company with those brands?
5. What are the current trends in the market, and how can your products contribute to those?

You'll next need to think about the following:

A) Company name
B) Product
C) Target market
D) Needs of your target market
E) Distinctiveness of your company

By filling in the blanks, you'll be well on defining a brand position.

[A – Company name] supplies [B – Product] to [C – Target market], looking for [D – Needs]. [A – Company name] distinguishes itself from competitors by [E – Distinctiveness].[5]

With positioning statements, it can be beneficial to lead with empathy, show that you understand your customers, keep it concise, embody your brand values, and be transparent.[6] Ultimately, everything starts with the customer, and you'll have to work backwards from their needs. There is a key video of Steve Jobs, where he dismisses the idea of working with engineers, looking at their technology and asking how they'll market it. He considers that strategy Inside Thinking, which is not how things work at Apple. Instead, they use Outside Thinking, starting with the customer experience and working backward. So, you can have a whiteboard filled with all the experiences consumers have with your brand, including how, where, when, and why they use it. Think about any possible friction points and determine if there are more effective ways to deliver the experience. Jobs says that when you start with the customer experience, you'll find new approaches and innovations that create passion and loyalty.[7]

WHAT IS A UNIQUE SELLING PROPOSITION (USP)?

A unique selling proposition is how you differentiate yourself from your competition. It will help you to attract and retain customers. The best USPs address a specific need experienced by your ideal customer. It should also emphasize what quality separates you from your competition and why they should choose you. Ideally, it should show you as a specialist in a certain area, something you're known for (instead of trying to be a generalist).

- You should be able to deliver your USP swiftly in an elevator pitch style.
- For [Your target audience]
- Who needs [Whatever product/service they need]
- [Name of your business]
- Is [position yourself as what you are]
- That [provides . . . describe the product or service]
- Unlike [how you're different from your competitors]
- [Your business name] . . . is the only e-commerce business in [wherever you're located] that caters specifically to [your target audience].
- You can use your USP in discussions, landing pages, and advertisements. Always emphasize the benefits of your service and address the pain points that your customers have rather than discuss product features.[8]

Examples of effective USPs

- **Amazon's** Unique Selling Proposition: providing access to a huge selection of goods at low prices, with fast delivery.
- **Netflix's** Unique Selling Proposition: provides quality entertainment to its users 24/7, a huge catalog of products for all tastes, and on-demand streaming without ads.
- **TikTok's** Unique Selling Proposition: enables creators to create a short-form mobile video so they can be creative, and people can have fun watching them.
- **Stripe's** Unique Selling Proposition: gives developers everything they need to manage online payments.

- **Robinhood's** Unique Selling Proposition: offers a platform for everyone to invest, with stocks as little as $1, from their smartphone. It breaks down barriers of a market usually closed off to the everyday person.[9]
- **Voodoo Doughnut's** Unique Selling Proposition: Doughnuts are so wacky that the wait is part of the experience. This shop in Portland, Oregon, makes its baked goods in a highly distinctive way that stands out from other doughnut shops. They have an extensive range, and to be unique, they also included Pepto-Bismol and NyQuil in their doughnuts, which got them into trouble with the FDA but helped the small doughnut shop go viral! It has pink rockabilly décor, cash-only, and late-night opening to make it a tourist attraction.
- **Osimum's** Unique Selling Proposition: All Hand-Made and All Local. Every garment is made by hand, with many makers in Boston. The company emphasizes its ethical production process and its product's durability.[10]

HOW TO WRITE A POSITIONING STATEMENT

A positioning statement is broader than your value proposition and is created after you've developed the value proposition. It will identify the primary customer benefits and why they need your product or service.

Think about:

1. Whom you serve
2. What value do you offer
3. How do you position your offer
4. Why you're in business
5. What makes you different from your competition

Create a vision board that is unique and memorable.

Remember to show the product's benefits rather than features. A vision board can help people connect with your vision rather than just a written document.

Keep your positioning statement brief.

It should be concise, 3–5 sentences.

Make it unique and memorable.

It should be unique to your company and the problems you solve. Show what is distinctive about your brand. Consumers should be able to see the value you offer.

Remain true to your business's core values.

These are the things that guide decisions in your business and create the culture of your organization.

Include what the brand delivers to consumers.

This should be your brand promise. Explain how your business solves your ideal customer's problems. Sometimes a product sells lifestyle, ideals, glamour, confidence, and style (consider cosmetics, clothing, and cars). It would be best if you showed you could meet their needs and solve their problems.[11]

Differentiate your business from the competition.

You need to be irresistible to your customers and show them why they should choose you over your competitors. There are many package carriers that people can choose from, but FedEx having the slogan, "When it absolutely, positively has to be there overnight," turned them into a global brand.[12] FedEx was certain they could make a promise and deliver on it. Show the gap your brand fills and how you do it better than anyone else.

Keep it simple.

It should be easy to understand, convincing, and engaging.

Consult a colleague.

It's always good to get a second opinion and ensure there's no jargon, acronyms, or things that are unclear to someone outside your company.

The four elements of a positioning statement

• **Target**

Who is your target? Who is your perfect/ideal customer, and what do they want? How can your product or service solve their problem? What motivates their buying decision? Why will they choose your business over competitors? It's important to remember that brands don't sell products; they sell benefits.[13]

- **Frame of reference**

This is what tells us what product category we're in. It's the basis for the point of difference. It can be conveyed by comparing your brand to a different one. It can also be communicated by showing what goal is achieved using the brand.[14]

- **Point of difference (USP)**

Points of difference are the areas where you can distinguish yourself from your competition, a unique selling point (USP)

- **Reason to believe**

This is why consumers in the target market should believe your brand's claims. What proof can you offer to support this?[15]

POSITIONING STATEMENT EXAMPLES

- **Coca-Cola**

"For individuals looking for high-quality beverages, Coca-Cola offers a wide range of the most refreshing options — each creates a positive experience for customers when they enjoy a Coca-Cola brand drink. Unlike other beverage options, Coca-Cola products inspire happiness and make a positive difference in customers' lives, and the brand is intensely focused on the needs of consumers and customers."[16]

Coca-Cola positions itself as popular worldwide, liked by alleged groups. Diet (and Zero) coke targets the niche segment of more health-conscious people. Coca-Cola associates happiness, positivity, and a good life with its products. There also is a strong association with Christmas (which many people view favorably) with the Coke Van imagery.[17] It appeals to customers' emotions!

- **Nike**

"For athletes needing high-quality, fashionable athletic wear, Nike provides customers with top-performing sports apparel and shoes made of the highest quality materials. Its products are the most advanced in athletic apparel because of Nike's commitment to innovation and investment in the latest technologies."

This is effective because it shows it's serving athletes but doesn't exclude anyone. Anyone who enjoys sport, whether as a hobby or a professional, can gain value from its products.

Another Nike one is: "At Nike, we're committed to creating a better, more sustainable future for our people, planet, and communities through the power of sport."

This works well because it shows its purpose, incorporates sustainability into its activewear, and breaks down barriers for athletes.[18]

- **Payhip**

"Payhip is an e-commerce platform that enables anyone to sell digital products or memberships directly to their fans and followers. You can embed Payhip directly into your website or use our storefront to sell your work. Payhip takes care of everything. We're an all-in-one e-commerce solution for creators."

This works well as a positioning statement because it communicates how easy it is to sell products with the platform. It frames it as an all-in-one, DIY e-commerce platform that works with all websites.

PERCEPTUAL MAPPING

Perceptual mapping can be an effective way to understand how your company, brand, or product is perceived by your competitors (also known as a positioning map). It shows you your position in the market![19]

Using the example of wanting to know what your customers think of your breakfast cereal compared to that of competitors. You could draw a cross and label the left-hand side as 'unhealthy,' the right as 'healthy,' the top as 'fun,' and the bottom as 'boring.' Then you would plot your cereal and your competitors' cereals on the map according to what your customers say.[20] You can use the tool to decide whether to go ahead with a potential product to see if it has a distinctive valuable market position. You can survey your customers and ask them to rate the products with a -5 and +5 range.

When you analyze your map, if your product doesn't have a distinct attractive position compared to competitors, it could be that your customers don't understand your USP. You'll need to tweak this and ensure that marketing and communication emphasize this. Depending on what parameters you're trying to measure, you may want to look at quality, price, packaging, and features. Does your customer's perception match yours? If it doesn't, you'll need to adjust your marketing strategy.

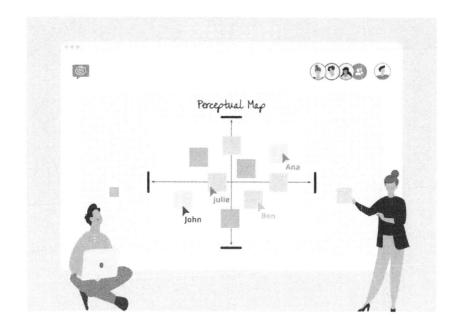

21

Perceptual maps are a four-square grid divided along the X and Y axes. The axes can correspond to competing values. You can pick two parameters. If you were selling shoes, you could look at design, style, quality, and functionality. If you were selling cereal, you could look at health values, sugar, fun/boring, and taste. If you were selling holidays, you could consider temperature, travel distance, culture, and safety. Next, list your competitors, aim for ten, rate them between 1–5, with one being the lowest and five the highest, then plot them on your graph. You should be able to see where you stand compared to your competitors and gaps in the market.

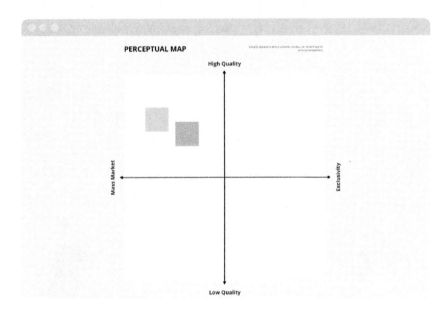

22

Creating a Perceptual Brand Positioning Map

An example using fast-food chains and outlets on the number of locations and the variety of menu items can be seen below:

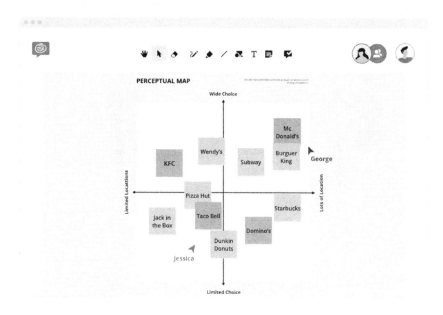

23

Pick your parameters and form a map.

An example would be to draw a cross where the north position has 'High Quality,' the south position has 'Low Quality,' the east position has 'High Price,' and the west position has 'Low Price.' [See image below.]

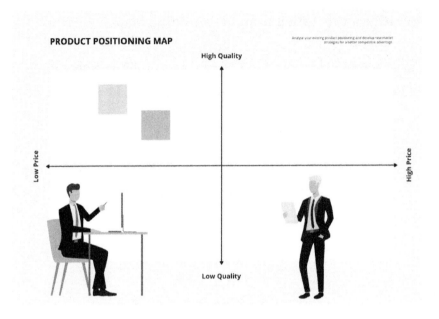

You would then position your product as meeting qualities that target a specific customer segment, their needs, and their lifestyle.

As a good follow-up activity after this to give you more insight, you could list competitors, rate competitors based on parameters on a scale of 1–5, then plot competitors on the map—to see where you stand in comparison to them.

Chapter Checklist:

1. Come up with a potential USP for your business.
2. Build a positioning statement around your USP.

3. Create a perceptual brand map and plot your business along with direct competitors.

Once you have fully positioned your business, you next need to determine a pricing strategy which we will cover in the next Chapter.

5

PRICING YOUR OFFER

> *"The moment you make a mistake in pricing, you're eating into your reputation or your profits."*
>
> — KATHARINE PAINE

We wanted to write this chapter because we know how long people agonize over how much to charge for their products and services. We've known people who have seemed to pluck a random figure out of the air (which we wouldn't recommend). The consequences of picking random figures are that you may not consider the true costs and end up making a loss or charge way too high, so any potential customer goes to your competitors instead. In contrast, others spend ages researching competitors' prices and price theirs accordingly but forget to consider what the product or service costs them regarding materials and time! Pricing is a vital part of your business, and you do have to consider many variables.

So, if you're struggling to know how much to charge for your products or service, this chapter is here to help you with tried and tested advice. The benefits of reading this chapter are that by the end, you should be able to identify a pricing strategy that works best for your business. You will know pricing options to make a sound, informed decision. You'll know case studies of other businesses' pricing models and be able to identify them with other companies. This may also give you insight into which strategy is the most sensible for you to apply.

This chapter discusses pricing strategies for three general online business models/offerings: physical, digital, and service-based. Pricing is important to get right; a Harvard study showed that a 1% improvement in pricing could equate to an 11% profit increase.[1]

WHAT IS A PRICING STRATEGY?

A pricing strategy is a way to determine how much you can charge for a product based on internal and external factors. It's based on supply and demand. The strategy may differ according to the industry, target customers, and cost of goods.

Price Elasticity of Demand

This is how a change in price affects consumer demand.[2] If customers still buy a product, regardless of the price increase, for example, cigarettes and fuel, it is called 'inelastic.' But other products have price fluctuations, such as food suppliers' prices or cinema tickets. Prices that fluctuate are called 'elastic.' Ideally, it's great if your product is inelastic.

How Should I Price My Products?

Cost-plus pricing would be where you:

1. Add up your variable costs (per product)

Variable costs do not remain the same month after month. They may differ depending on how many products you sell. They can include production supplies, raw materials, packing, credit card fees, etc. How much does each product cost you? If you order products, this should be easy to work out. To make products, you must consider raw materials, labor, and overheads. If you buy in bulk or bundles, you need to determine how many you can make out of this. Don't forget your own time; remember to work this out as an hourly salary you want to be paid and work out how many products you can make in that time. You need a price that your customer will pay consistently. You can consider the cost of the goods, production time, packaging, promotional materials, shipping, and affiliate commissions.

In times of inflation, it is worth keeping a close check and regularly monitoring variable costs because prices can increase quickly. You may need to look around for better deals on raw materials and credit cards to ensure you always get the most for your money. It is worth always factoring a bit of 'wiggle room' into your variable costs because things can crop up unexpectedly, or a supplier you've previously used could cease to trade, and you need to use a more expensive one—so factor this in and assume things will cost a little more so that you are prepared for economic uncertainty. When there is inflation, customers may not buy as much of your product as they previously have because things will be tighter for them financially. If you don't order as much in bulk, this can impact your pricing costs, making them more expensive. Keep all the above in mind, and regularly check these costs.

2. Consider your profit margin

It would be best to consider what percentage profit margin you're happy with. It could be around 20% on top of your variable costs. You haven't included fixed costs yet, so these must also be considered. You'll need to look at the overall market and ensure that what you're asking is reasonable compared to the market. If you're double the price of your competitors, you may find it hard to get sales. Research a profit margin based on your growth goals, what is normal in the market, and your costs.

3. Don't forget about fixed costs

You pay fixed costs—regardless of whether you sell 10 or 1,000 items. The aim is that these fixed costs are covered by your sales too. Fixed costs could cover insurance, rent, salaries, loan payments, and utilities. It's worth considering how many products you must sell to break even.[3]

When determining the price of something, you can use product pricing calculators that may help. You can find these free on many different sites. You can experiment with what percentage of profit you'd like to receive until you find a price that works for you and your customer. Observe sales data, too, and adjust your prices accordingly.[4]

Other Basic Pricing Strategies

For physical products

- **Competition-Based Pricing Strategy in Marketing**

This looks at the current market rate to develop a cost for the product or service. It doesn't consider cost or consumer demand. It would use your competitor's prices as a benchmark. If you plan on selling an item for $400, but your competitor sells it at $375, you may want to lower your price to match theirs. You may price the same, slightly below or slightly above your competitors. Buyers want the best value, which isn't always the cheapest. If you offer something your competitors don't, this can put you in a good position (customer service, returns policy, loyalty scheme).

- **Premium Pricing**

This is also known as luxury pricing or prestige pricing. By giving your product a high price, it is done to suggest luxury, quality, and high value; they are sold to high-income individuals.[5] It is done to influence the perception of the product rather than being a true reflection of the product cost. It falls into brand awareness. Some items in the fashion sector are given premium pricing, such as designer labels for clothing and accessories. Creating a luxury brand or lifestyle to accompany premium pricing would be best. While pricing your product high may seem counterintuitive, it can create a feeling of exclusivity and status in the buyers who can afford it.[6] However this is definitely a hard strategy for beginners and may require a lot of initial capital to make it take off.

For Digital Products

Digital products may include digital books, online courses, or software. There is no tangible product; working out a unit cost may be harder. But when deciding on a price, you can think about your brand, your industry, and what value your product provides.

- **Value-Based Pricing Strategy**

Warren Buffett's quote, 'Price is what you pay. Value is what you get' is a reminder that when you price your product or service, you must look at things from your customer's perspective. They need to think that what they're paying gives them good value for money. This is a value-based pricing strategy. When you try to think like a customer, consider the product's necessity, quality, and usefulness.

- **Freemium Pricing Strategy**

A freemium price strategy is one where people get a free service (it may be basic) but then pay for upgrades or access to more features.[7] Software companies often use it. We would advise against a 'freemium' pricing model because it suggests people wouldn't get value from a product (or else they'd be willing to pay), and you're not taking money from the customers who would have been willing to pay but are now using it for free. A trial for a limited time is OK, as this does build trust with the customer, and the product needs to speak for itself and be something valuable that the customer then decides they can't live without. Generally, freemium prices grow incrementally depending on customer needs.

For Services

If you're offering a service rather than a tangible product, you must ensure that you deliver the service to the best of your ability and produce high-quality work.

- **Value-Based Pricing**

This is where companies base their product on what customers are willing to pay. The company will set its price around customer interest and data.[8] It can make customers loyal to you. But it would be best to work hard to be in tune with your customers and be prepared to vary prices accordingly.

- **Project-Based Pricing Strategy**

This charges a flat project fee, regardless of the work hours involved. Contractors, freelancers, consultants, and others who provide services often work this way. The price can be based on the deliverables of the project and what value they have to the customer. When you point out the benefits to the customer, this can make a steep investment seem worthwhile.

- **Hourly Pricing Strategy**

This is also known as rate pricing and is typically used by free-lancers, contractors, and consultants who provide services. This way of working trades time for money rather than valuing efficiency. If you have a lot of quick projects, hourly pricing can encourage customers to work with you rather than a high project-based price.

REAL LIFE PRICING STRATEGY EXAMPLES

1. Chicago Cubs

People who regularly watch these games will be familiar with ticket prices fluctuating. If you book your ticket six weeks in advance, this will be a different price to booking on the day. If it's a holiday when the game takes place, this will be more expensive too. This is an example of **dynamic pricing**.

2. AWAY Luggage

This is an example of **premium pricing**, where the luggage has a hefty price tag. But it has unique branding, and for people who buy into the name of the product, for them it has value.[9]

3. Shopify

This e-commerce platform employs a **competitive pricing strategy** where its prices are often lower than other competitors on the market. They have three price versions of their product that offer different things depending on customer requirements.

4. Courtney Samuel Events

This offers a **project-based pricing** strategy by offering different wedding coordination packages. It can offer a fixed fee for the project by focusing on the value of the outcome, a stress-free day for the bride and groom. Having a 'fixed fee,' the customer can pay this and not worry about tracking how many work hours have been used, checking invoices, etc.

5. INBOUND

This is an example of value-based pricing. Customers are given a range of ticket prices they can choose from at different levels, allowing them to pick what experience they want depending on their perceived value of the event.

FINDING THE RIGHT STRATEGY FOR YOU

Think about the approximate price of your product or service. How much does it cost? What is the demand for it? Are your markets geographical? What are your operating costs? Will you need inventories? Do you predict demand fluctuations? Consider competitive advantages and concerns. Think about demographic data. Consider the lifetime value of your product, what the customer is willing to pay, and customer pain points. What problem does this solve for your customer? Look back at previous pricing history (if you have any) and what has worked well for you. Look at your competitors and decide whether to beat their price or value. You could find 3–5 competitors by doing online research or looking at local businesses. You could also speak with potential customers about what price they would pay for your brand, product, or service. You could ask friends and family or survey this.[10] You need to pay attention to basic financial information and consider the margins. You can experiment with pricing strategies to find what works and be aware that you may have to change this initially.

If you don't price a product properly, it could result in customer dissatisfaction (your product needs to live up to expectations), low profit margins (you need to be covering more than just your cost and can use cost-based pricing with your desired margin on top of this), low sales (if you're over-priced), or a perception of you being a 'bargain brand,' where people will never want to pay full price for your product.

Chapter Checklist:

1. Based on your niche product/service, choose a pricing strategy that best aligns with your overall goals and brand.
2. Conduct a basic analysis of your costs and competitive prices to give you a benchmark for setting your prices.

6

BRANDING IN A NUTSHELL

> "*A brand is no longer what we tell the consumer it is – it is what consumers tell each other it is.*"
>
> — SCOTT COOK

This chapter continues from Chapter 4 but provides a more in-depth look at branding and brand strategy. It's by building brand awareness and loyalty that you'll contribute to creating a successful business. Jeff Bezos, the CEO of Amazon, states that "a brand for a company is like a reputation for a person. You earn a reputation by trying to do hard things well." He also states, "Your brand is what other people say about you when you're not in the room."[1]

In this chapter, we will address the topic of what a brand strategy is; this will help you to understand why a brand strategy is of crucial importance to your business. It's not something that is a trendy jargon phrase. It's not something that is just a 'tick-box exercise.' A good brand strategy will give your business a solid identity, meaning customers relate to your brand, stay loyal, and repeat business with you. A good brand strategy can help make your business successful and make it more profitable, and sustainable.

This chapter will teach you about twelve different brand archetypes and help you decide which most strongly aligns with your business. You can put together a brand style guide that covers: identity, story, voice, design, and values. By the end of this chapter, you will have gained much greater clarity about how you want to brand your business and the reasons why.

WHAT IS BRAND STRATEGY?

Brand strategy is made up of different components. Having a clear strategy is important to help direct one's business. Things like your voice to your audience and the values that drive you forward form part of your brand. So, the strategy is about building an identity and favorability with customers. A brand strategy is planning how to present your business to the world. It will keep the brand at the forefront of everything you do so the brand is memorable to customers[2]. A brand strategy has been compared to the foundations of a house; you need this in place to build from.[3] There are five key parts to a brand strategy:

1. **Voice** –the words and phrases you communicate with on your website, social media, or products. This will help you to connect to your customers and show your personality and values.[4]

2. **Design** – this is your brand's visual appearance. You must carefully consider the colors you use, the font, and the photo style, which will likely emotionally connect you to your customer. Your design will appear and feature on everything, including labels, packaging, webpage, etc. Your design can differentiate you from your competitors.

3. **Values** – this is why your company exists and is about what is most important to you. Is there a solution that your business provides? Clear values will help you make decisions and collaborate with others, depending on whether they align with your strong values.

4. **Story** – what is your origin story? Core beliefs? Values and purpose of your company? This will explain why you exist, what you believe in, your inspiration and motivation, and allow your customers to get to know you better.

5. **Vibe** – is a customer's feeling about your company based on your social media, website, and packaging. You could have a playful, entertaining vibe, a serious educational one, or a funny one. Customers associate the feeling of 'energy' or 'calm' with your business and products[5].

It is good for customers to feel you have moral values, a voice that captures your brand, and a design that shows the business's personality.

Why Is Developing a Branding Strategy Important?

We feel like we know and love the brands we connect with. When you have a strong brand, customers will be loyal to you, be aware of you, and return to you for repeat business. A good brand will help you get word-of-mouth marketing and referrals.[6] Your business may be forgettable if you don't develop a branding strategy. There will often be an 'archetype' to the brand we connect with; we'll explore twelve different archetypes below so you can decide which 'archetype' you want your brand to represent. The archetypes each help to build an emotional connection with your audience and help to build loyalty. You'll fondly view brands whom you've built a real connection with and may have memories of, for example, specific meals family members make you or playing with Lego, perhaps as a child. When you build such a connection to a brand, alternative brands won't suffice.[7] When customers build a connection to your brand, they'll keep coming back and purchasing more.

THE 5 ESSENTIAL ELEMENTS OF AN EFFECTIVE BRAND STRATEGY

1. Brand Identity – the 12 brand archetypes

Archetypes are personifications of a behavior. They're like a character who acts in a certain way with whom you can identify. Everyone is different and has different values that matter to them, and this is something brands can play on to appeal to specific market segments. When you have your brand aligned with an archetype, this allows you to make a deeper connection with your audience, and it allows you to differentiate yourself from your competitors. According to Harvard Professor Gerald Zaltman, 95% of consumers' purchasing decisions are subconscious; these archetypes connect with people subconsciously, and people recognize them.

There are well-known characters from literature and film that we can immediately fit into the twelve archetypes, such as Indiana Jones (the explorer), Yoda (the sage), and Maximum from Gladiator (the Hero). So archetypes can help your brand because they are memorable; they'll immediately convey a meaning your customers can relate to and identify with. When you choose an archetype, you can't appeal to everyone; you are trying to appeal to a particular market segment. Brands with one distinct archetype increase value by 97% more than those confused brands. So, you need to identify your customer's personality and align it with a brand archetype (Houraghan, 2018, online).

- **The Innocent** – this is about safety.

With this archetype, the customer likes a simple, straightforward life that is optimistic, honest, humble, unadulterated, and pure. Brands that use this 'innocent' archetype include Innocent fruit smoothies, Aveeno, and Dove. The customer's personality is easygoing, not one that holds grudges; they see the beauty in everyone and can appreciate inner beauty. They want to be happy. They have good, pure, young, optimistic, moral, and loyal traits.[8] The brand strategy is to show a wholesome virtuous life and to make people feel good. You must be simple, honest, and positive to appeal to 'innocent' personalities with your brand. The brand should be seen as trustworthy, reliable, and honest. There could be some nostalgia associated with the brand. This brand strategy is good for beauty and skin products, organic produce, and fresh food.

- **The Regular Guy or Gal (also known as Everyman)** – is about belonging and connection[9].

Branding is about people identifying as similar to someone portrayed as friendly, humble, and down-to-earth. Well-known brands that use this archetype include Lynx, Target, Home Depot, eBay, and IKEA. This person fits in with society but doesn't stand out. This archetype is about inclusion, connection, and togetherness. The audience is people who feel 'normal.' It's often used for home or family life brands. It can be used for comfort foods, everyday apparel, or vehicles.

- **The Hero** – this is about mastery.

This person is honest, candid, brave, and has determination and grit. Existing brands that use this archetype include Adidas, Nike, BMW, Duracell, and FedEx. A strategy would be to become stronger and better and prove people wrong. You want to inspire them to feel empowered and help improve the world and solve problems. Color palettes may include black, white, and grey.

- **The Outlaw** – this is about liberation.

This person believes rules are made to be broken. This personality will go against authority figures. They are disruptive, rebellious, and combative. Existing brands that use this archetype include Virgin, Harley Davidson, and Diesel. A strategy would be to denounce the status quo, disrupt, shock, and pave the way for change. The color palettes may include browns and creams.

- **The Explorer** – this is about freedom.

The brand voice should be exciting, fearless, and daring. Brands that use the explorer archetype include The North Face, Jeep, Red Bull, and Patagonia. People with explorers' personalities put themselves outside their comfort zone; they are brave, adventurous, and love new challenges. A brand strategy for the archetype could be focused on celebrating the journey and acknowledging modern confinements. By acknowledging modern confinements, you challenge the person to break out.

This personality takes risks and desires excitement. This personality type generally sees the outdoors as a place of freedom to explore. This archetype may be used for extreme sports, outdoor equipment, SUVs, and adventure travel.

- **The Creator** – this is about innovation.

Imagination is used to create new things. It's about being inspired, daring, and provocative. The brand message is about seeing potential everywhere and discovering originality. Brands that use the creator archetype include Lego, Apple, Crayola, and Adobe. There is a drive to express oneself, have a vision, unlock imagination, and pursue originality. To attract creative people to your brand, you want to celebrate creativity and inspire them to express themselves by giving them the tools, means, and freedom of choice. The creator archetype will be used in the arts, design, IT, marketing, and writing.

- **The Ruler** – this is about control.

For this personality, power is super important. The brand voice needs to be commanding, refined, and articulate. Brands like Microsoft, Barclays, Louis Vuitton, Rolex, and Mercedes Benz use this branding archetype. Rulers want to feel like they are superior and VIPs; they may have the desire to create order from chaos. If you want to use ruler archetype branding, your customers must feel at the pinnacle of success and exclusivity. This archetype branding is often used for luxury cars, watches, hotels, formal wear, and any luxury item.

- **The Magician** – this is about power.

This person wants something mystical, informed, and reassuring; a transformational journey. Existing brands using this archetype include Coca-Cola, Disney, Apple, and Dyson. This person strives to make dreams come true; the only limit is imagination. A strategy would be developing a vision to show it can be lived. Color palettes may include blues and purples.

- **The Lover** – is about intimacy, sensuality, empathy, and soothing.

A brand strategy is to reaffirm the beauty and to provide the red-carpet treatment. The color palette may include sage green, pink, and burgundy. For branding, you need to make the person feel attractive and appreciated or make them desire connection and intimacy. This archetype is often used with fragrances, indulgent food, or travel and by brands like Victoria's Secret, Godiva chocolate, or Marie Claire.

- **The Caregiver** – this is about service, caring for, and protecting others.

The brand voice is caring, warm, and reassuring. Many charities, such as UNICEF and WWF, use this brand and other companies, like Campbell's Soup, Johnson & Johnson, and Heinz. This will be a desire to care for others in need. It's about being supportive, helpful, and providing a service. Putting others before yourself. If you're a brand that provides care, you must make your customers feel secure, protected, and cared for.

This archetype could be used for care providers, education, not-for-profits, and hospitals.

- **The Jester** – is about enjoyment, joy, fun-loving, and pleasure.

The voice for this archetype needs to be playful, impulsive, fun-loving, and optimistic. It is very much about seizing the day and having a childlike quality. The brand strategy should portray having a good time and ideally make people laugh. It could be used for sweets, beer, or child services. Ben and Jerry's and IKEA use this archetype in their branding.

- **The Sage** – this is about understanding.

The brand voice should be knowledgeable, assured, and guiding. Your brand should portray how education is valuable to gain wisdom. It is about intelligence, expertise, and information. Brands that use the sage archetype include Google, BBC, Philips, and the University of Oxford. The brand strategy should show people how to acquire wisdom and encourage life-long learning. With your strategy, you need to communicate intelligently using good vocabulary. Don't simplify or dumb down your message. Types of businesses that use the sage archetype include media and news networks, schools and universities, consultancies, and search engines.

It is possible to 'mix' archetypes, but you need to do so carefully so that you're not confusing, and your lead/core archetype needs to represent at least 70% of your brand personality.[10] If you do a mix, ensure that the 30% archetype you use is well used to differentiate you from other brands. When you present a brand archetype to customers, you're letting them know that they are the same as you, or they can aspire to be like you, or you can guide them, or you're reassuring them that they can be great and achieve all they want to in life.

CREATE A BRAND STYLE GUIDE

Creating a comprehensive brand style guide that covers your brand identity, story, voice, design, and values can be useful.

Brand Identity

Pick your brand archetype and be clear about its opinions about your market and the wider industry. Use keywords. Identify the archetype's attitude toward life. A tone of voice and writing style captures these opinions and attitudes. Pick certain vocab that will help to evoke your archetype. Look for synonyms of these vocab words to use in your brand guidelines. Ensure that your brand visually represents the personality with the colors you use, the typography, and the images. The more detail you can include in your brand personality, the stronger it will connect with customers and be memorable to them. The key things to focus on when creating a brand style are the look, feel, tone, attitude, opinions, and vocabulary. Ensuring this aligns with an archetype (or a 70% main archetype, 30% another archetype to help with differentiation). Once you have your archetype, you must create a brand story.

Brand Story

Research by Uri Hasson has shown that people are twenty-two times more likely to recall a story than a fact![11] People don't just want information; they want to be taken on a journey. With your brand archetype character, be sure to delve into this. You need to create intrigue and be authentic. What is the background of your brand archetype? What are its future goals? What is the journey like? Brands need to connect to customers on a human level. Using an archetype's personality can help connect with your audience and show how your brand differs.

You need to understand why you're running your own business. It's sensible to map out your vision so that you have something to work toward, and putting this in writing will bring you more success. Whenever you have a business decision, ask yourself if it will help you work toward your vision. Dream big and consider where you'd like to be in five years. Break your overall vision down into manageable goals.[12] Remember to share your story everywhere.

Brand Voice

You need to define your market and focus exclusively on them. A key example is how the brand Man Crates has a strong sense of humor. They've created a memorable buyer experience on their website filled with anticipation. Man Crates uses storytelling to build anticipation and convince people they've found the perfect gift.[13] Their story is easy to visualize, builds anticipation and excitement, and is fun. Making people laugh and enjoy themselves is important. Man Crates uses humorous male stereotypes in their YouTube videos, targeting women who can identify with the males in the videos.

Brand Design

When considering brand design, you can think about the role of art in branding, a logo, the colors you decide to associate your brand with, the font you use, the shapes you use, and a tagline. Because there is a wealth of choices of different brands for people, having a trustworthy brand is essential. When you're considering your brand design, you could decide to draw upon science (generating insight, measuring performance, being data-driven), art (creativity), or craft (management and execution).[14] You can think about your name, a trademarked symbol, or the music associated with your brand. If you think of McDonald's brand design, its golden arches are instantly recognizable.[15] The NBA logo has the slogan always used with it: "Where Amazing Happens." Making your logo stand out from others with its design, color, or font would be best. When you have a video or radio advertisement, you can consider what music or jingle you want to be associated with your brand. Once you have a recognizable brand design, you need to disseminate it widely; you can utilize podcasts, have partnerships with other brands, do guest blogs, advertise on social media, use giveaways, use hashtags, and like or comment on social media using your brand name.

Logo, Color, Font, Shapes, and Tagline – Your logo needs to summarize what your brand stands for. Your logo will have colors, shapes, images, and fonts. Comparing the Coca-Cola and Pepsi logos, Coca-Cola uses a darker red, which suggests it's classic and serious. Pepsi uses red, white, and blue seeking alignment with the American flag. Coca-Cola's font is swirly, again showing it's classic, original, and evokes nostalgia. Pepsi's font is more minimalistic and modern. Coca-Cola has a swooping shape under it which looks like a gift ribbon and creates associations with Christmas and special memories. Pepsi's red, white, and blue circle resembles a friendly smile.

Taglines are short statements that quickly put across your key branding strategy message. Here are some well-known brief taglines you'll probably have heard of: McDonald's: I'm Lovin' It (which is written in the first person showing how much they love it and dropping the 'g' off the word 'Loving' makes it casual, informal and fun). Ford: Go Further (is about succeeding with one's goals/dreams and exploring new places). Nike: Just Do It (is full of motivation and seize the moment). Burger King: Be Your Way (emphasizes autonomy and having choice over your life) and Apple: Think Different (is about daring to be creative and think outside the box to come up with new solutions, it's entrepreneurial).[16]

Brand Values

Your brand values are the principles and ideals that state what you stand for, and these principles will drive you.[17] Your values should be built around your purpose as a company. Your clients will share these same brand values. It's good to share your brand values on the about page of your website. Your values are really important and not just a tick-box exercise. They should permeate every bit of your website. Good brand values are what can turn a one-off customer into a loyal one who returns to you time and time again.[18] Your ideals and values could be protecting the environment, diversity, solidarity, or transparency. These will form a key part of your brand's identity. Your values must reflect what is truly important to the company, and you must honestly care about them and do all you can to implement them. Your values are your guiding beliefs, and your guiding principles are how you will follow this through. So, if your value is 'transparency,' then your guiding principle would be good communication with customers about your products' origin and manufacturing. Also, having very transparent prices in detail.

Tesla's values are about doing the best, taking risks, respect, constant learning, and environmental consciousness. Nike's values are inspiration, innovation, inclusiveness, and being distinctive. Lego values are fun, learning, creativity, care, and quality. Suppose you're unsure about defining your brand's core values. In that case, you could brainstorm with your team, survey your customers, and analyze your competition to see if there's an opportunity or space for you to offer something they aren't. You should ideally have 3–5 main values. You should have 1–2 guiding principles per brand value. You can include the values and guiding principles in your brand guidelines. Stick to these values at all times and let them define your brand.

Chapter Checklist:

Create a brand guideline for your business, including the five essential elements mentioned above:

1. Brand identity
2. Brand story
3. Brand voice
4. Brand design
5. Brand values

The key takeaways from this chapter include the following:

1. Brand strategy is about creating an identity and winning customer favorability. It would help if you planned to achieve this using voice, design, values, story, and vibe.
2. When you have a brand strategy, customers will connect with you, be loyal and return for repeat business. Without a brand strategy, you'll be forgotten.
3. Twelve archetypes can help build an emotional connection with your audience. Purchasing decisions of 95% of consumers are subconscious. People connect with these archetypes subconsciously. If you have a distinct archetype, you'll increase the value of your business by 97% more than if your archetype is confused.
4. If you mix archetypes, have a mix of 70% for your lead/core archetype and a 30% archetype to differentiate your brand.
5. Create a brand style guide focusing upon IDENTITY (choose an archetype), STORY (this makes your brand

twenty-two times more memorable), VOICE (for example, could be humorous if appropriate to your brand), DESIGN (art, logo, colors, font, shapes, and tagline), VALUES (ideals, guiding principles, 77% of customers buy from brands that share their values).

The next chapter will look at developing a winning marketing strategy by creating an effective digital marketing plan, including various tactics and strategies.

7

LET'S GET MARKETING

Once you get your product and your clients right, you cannot disregard a good marketing strategy. You need to be able to attract customers to your website and raise awareness of your product or service. It's okay to not get it right from the first day, but you should try different strategies until you find out what works best for your target audience.

Your marketing (or lack of it) can make or break your business; people need to know about your product or service and how they can purchase it. They need to know the benefits of it and, ideally, form an emotional connection to your brand. It's perfect if your ideal customer can view you as an expert in the area connected to your business and wants to gain information from you.

As a new startup business, you may feel that you have the skills and experience to run your business, but you may not know where to start with marketing. You may not be technically minded or know how to create or optimize websites. When you start a business, it is hard to do everything, all of the administration, everything financial, HR jobs, and the marketing/social media side; this is why bigger businesses have specialists in these areas.

This chapter will give you the benefits of being able to do these marketing tasks yourself, or at least raise your awareness of what marketing tasks 'can' be conducted, and then you could get a company with expertise in these areas to do these for you.

By the end of the chapter, you will have the basic knowledge/insights/tools to create your own business marketing plan and especially to know what the bigger picture is, why it's important to have a business marketing plan, and the reasons behind it, plus guidance to start creating this today.

HOW TO CREATE YOUR ONLINE BUSINESS MARKETING PLAN STEP-BY-STEP

Besides helping you stay on schedule and budget, a marketing plan is essential to effectively nurture your customers, improve your business's bottom line, and increase the ROI of your efforts. I recommend you get your plan documented because research has shown that top marketers were 414% more likely to report success when they documented their strategy[1] and tracked their initiatives against their results to derive learnings to be implemented in their future initiatives. Like many people, knowing where to start to create a plan can be hard. Following the clear steps below will help you:

Step 1: Assess your current business situation

You could use a SWOT analysis (Strengths, Weaknesses, Opportunities, and Threats) to assess your current business situation.[2] The SWOT analysis will help you work out the areas you're doing well and the areas you could improve. Any areas that need improvement can be perceived as an opportunity. You could also do a SWOT analysis of your competitors to analyze their marketing, what they do well, etc. The Pareto principle suggests that 80% of your business will come from 20% of your customers. This is one of the most important reasons to have a strong marketing plan in place—to create customer engagement and an audience to get repeat and loyal customers rather than attract someone new.

Step 2: Set a budget

You need to clearly understand what money you have available to invest in marketing. New businesses spend 12–20% of their gross revenue on marketing, which can reduce to 6–12% when established.[3] While this can seem like a lot of money, you should always keep in mind the ROI that this can generate with the right marketing plan. Even a very small budget can get your business to the next level. Break down the full costs of your marketing plan, in as much detail, with as much accuracy as possible. Once you start to put your plan into action, keep checking your costs against your plan.[4]

While setting a financial budget, it can also be wise to budget your time and assess how much available time you can dedicate to spend on marketing each week.

Step 3: Outline your marketing goals

Once you have an idea of your strengths, areas for opportunity, and a financial/time budget, you can write your marketing goals.

- **Marketing and Sales goals**

Your goals should be SMART (Specific, Measurable, Attainable, Relevant, and Time-Bound). An example of a SMART would be to increase website traffic by 4% over the next six months . Other marketing goals could be building an online presence, generating leads (this could be a contact who is a prospective customer, hoping they will become a future client), increasing brand awareness, and connecting, engaging with, and growing your online audience.[5]

- **Brand Awareness**

It would be best to communicate regularly, ensuring that customers know what your brand stands for so that they are fully familiar with your values and mission and that you are in people's minds when they want to purchase if your values align with theirs. It's a good idea to have personalized communication.

- **Expansion**

Expansion is about how you will grow your business in the future. Expansion is about your plans to scale up and develop. Some questions you can ask yourself to determine the direction you will expand are: What are your plans for your business? Where do you see yourself in a year? Three years? Five years? Is your business currently local, national, or international? Do you have physical premises and, if so, would you like this to expand to further physical premises? What different (but related) areas could you expand your business into so that your business grows and develops?

- **Customer Retention and Acquisition**

You want to acquire new customers and retain (keep) all the customers you get. There are various strategies you can implement that will help to acquire and retain customers. It's about creating a seamless customer experience, from issue to resolution. Some strategies you can implement are as follows: Ensure your website has information that is easy to find, that the site is easily searchable, that it showcases your products, and that customers can get answers to any questions.[6] You can create a loyalty program to drive repeat purchases and increase engagement. If you create a loyalty program, to ensure success, make the customer feel exclusive, encourage participation, and keep the rewards attainable.[7] You can offer incentives to customers with promotions, free shipping, and free returns, and reward your top customers with a surprise and delight gift.

Step 4: Identify your target audience

- **Target market**

Describe your ideal customers in detail. Find out the size of the market, the demographics, unique traits, and trends.[8] Knowing your target audience will help you develop your marketing plan because, as an example, Gen-Z audiences probably would not be reached as easily through print ads.[9] Consider your current customers and whether there's a target group you aren't currently reaching. Understand what your customers buy from you and why (their motivation). Do you know what influenced their purchasing decision (whether they do or don't buy, what prompted them to, or prevented them from doing so?). How do your customers find out about you? Where do your customers spend time online? What are your competitors' customers like?

Step 5: Determine your marketing tactics

- **Competitive advantage**

A competitive advantage is the combination of marketing elements that sets your business apart. It's about finding the unique benefit that customers get when they purchase a product or service from you. There are questions you can ask yourself to help determine and pinpoint your competitive advantage so that you can market it. What gives the product or service you provide an advantage over your competition? Is your product better quality? Is it a lower price? Do you provide outstanding customer service? Is your product environmentally friendly? Or a locally sourced product?[10]

- **Building trust and loyalty**

You can do different things when building a brand that can influence customers' perceptions of your brand. Staff uniforms, where your products are made, and your return policy can add 'trust' from customers in your brand. You can encourage customers to leave reviews. Avoid shortcuts or clickbait tactics. Don't remove all negative feedback; respond politely, take ownership of the problem, and remedy it. Treat your customers as you would a friend. Offer loyalty programs. Offer a high level of customer service, with high standards on speed and quality. Always deliver what you have promised. Show and adhere to your company values. Be transparent. Ensure that you solve customers' problems. Ask for customer feedback. Be reachable to customers and respond to inquiries swiftly. Cultivate relationships.

Step 6: Put together an action plan that prioritizes tasks

You need to write a list of all you want to do with marketing, then prioritize the list. You can download free action plan templates from here: If you prefer to work in Word, this is a Word document:

https://business.vic.gov.au/tools-and-templates/marketing-action-plan-template.

If you prefer to work in Excel, here is an Excel spreadsheet:

https://ganttpro.com/marketing-action-plan-template/.

You can download many other free plans online, so it's worth looking for one that appeals to your style. I would advise you to have a table to keep track of the following:

1. Your tactics/initiatives
2. Timeline
3. Goals
4. Results

The table will help you track your results against your goals and then adjust your future initiatives if these don't meet your expectations.[11]

An action plan can comprise a sales plan, a marketing action plan, and aligning your goals and strategies. Read the paragraphs below to learn more about these.

- **Sales plan**

Knowing how your customers will buy products or services from you would be best. So consider documenting how you will sell your product or service to customers. Will this be retail, wholesale, or via an online store? Next, please write down your customers' steps when they purchase. For online stores, it's worth checking these steps to see if you can slimline them and make it much easier for customers to buy. Are there currently any obstacles in their way? It's worth considering your sales plan as part of an action plan because your marketing will hopefully ultimately guide people to make the final purchase. You don't want 'how' people pay to be a barrier to them following through on a sale. There is a free sales plan template to download here as a PDF, Word Doc, or Google Doc:

https://fitsmallbusiness.com/sales-plan-template/.

This format will help you assemble everything. Other templates are available online, too; some will request your email address in return for the template. Conduct a search and find one that suits your style.

- **Marketing action plan**

It would help if you had a plan for achieving your marketing and sales goals. If there are specific marketing channels you'll use, put these in a list, such as online advertising, radio ads, billboards, etc. Explain your pricing strategy and think about promotions. What support is given to customers after their purchase? Ensure your labeling is legally compliant with government regulations.

- **Align your online marketing goals, strategies, and tactics**

Outline your goals for the next year. Your goals could include increasing your email subscribers, growing your market share, or increasing your sales by a specific percentage. These are all specific, measurable goals.[12] Constantly measure and update your plan, ensure that your goals, strategies, and tactics align, and ensure you get a positive ROI. Ensure that your marketing efforts are effective.

TYPES OF DIGITAL MARKETING STRATEGIES

As part of your marketing plan discussed above, you can employ various types of digital marketing strategies. Suppose consumers want to learn about a business. In that case, they search for this online rather than anywhere else, so it's important that your online offering adequately gives consumers the information they require in the best possible way. E-commerce users are predicted to grow to almost 274 million by 2025.[13] If you have little experience in online marketing, choosing which digital marketing strategy to use may seem overwhelming, but we are here to help you navigate this. We will now go through different digital marketing strategies to help you achieve the main end goal of a marketing plan, benefiting your business by raising brand awareness and building a pipeline of leads that convert into sales. You can do several things to make this process less of a headache, especially if you don't have a large budget or lack time or staff to help.

Search Engine Optimization (SEO)

SEO is what makes your business visible online to potential customers. Utilizing SEO will help search engines find your website through organic search engine results (non-paid). You should start using it from the beginning because it is worth implementing, but it will take time to build and appear higher up in the rankings due to competition.

Bots scroll the Internet to find and show the most relevant content to internet users using keywords; SEO may give your website the chance to optimize content to meet criteria, so your website ranks more highly in the search engine results, and you get more warm leads and potential sales. SEO determines whether your content will show on a SERP (search engine results page).[14]

Three key SEO benefits are getting more leads, increasing sales, and continually generating traffic. Fifty-three percent of website traffic comes from organic search, five times more than pay-per-click (PPC) advertising and ten times more than social media.[15] Thirty-three percent of your revenue should come from search engine results pages. This strategy takes time but is better than paid advertising in the long run.[16]

Suppose you're not ranking as highly in Google as you'd like to. In that case, this may be due to relevant keywords (and their placement on your site), the length of your content, high-quality content relevant to your target audience, how fast your page loads, and how often you post content, plus other factors. Google will try to find the best information, so if someone is looking for a hair salon in Lincoln, Nebraska, it isn't helpful if they find one in Lincoln, UK.

- **Optimize your website (and localize it)**

Website optimization is where you use tools, strategies, and experiments to improve the performance of your website, drive more traffic to it, increase conversions (of people purchasing your product or service), and grow your revenue.[17] Website localization is when you refine and optimize web content using culture, language and flow to give users the most useful and relevant experience; you can consider the nuances of the target region. You can also adapt the products, services, and marketing strategies to meet a particular local market's needs and preferences.[18] Localization connects to SEO mentioned above because your keywords can be localized. If you lack expertise or time, you could consult an agency or freelancer specializing in web design to optimize your website for you. You could find a freelancer on places like Upwork, Codeable, or Freelancer. Whether it is yourself or a freelancer who optimizes and localizes your website, ideally, you should have several social media accounts with all your linked social media icons and a newsletter sign-up call to action on all website pages (usually in the top right corner or the footer of each page).[19] As mentioned in the previous paragraph, your keywords and key phrases should be based on local SEO; you can get local SEO insights using tools like Google Analytics, Google Trends, and Google Search Console.[20]

- **Update title tags and meta descriptions**

Title tags and meta descriptions tell search engines and users what your site is about. They describe the content on each website page and can be used as a 'hook' for your advertising in the search engine results.[21] Ensure your keywords, meta description, page titles, and H1 tags are in the correct places on your website. Page titles should have an H1 tag; most content management systems do this automatically.[22]

A title tag is the 60 characters search engines use to see on the search engine results page (SERP). If you can, use a title tag relevant to your brand and location, and ensure it is less than 60 characters.

The meta description will increase your click-through rates because it lets consumers know which information they will find on your website.[23] Meta descriptions can entice people to visit; these should be limited to 150 characters.[24]

Your site should load swiftly; there is a Google Page Insight Tool, and your site should score 85 or better. If there's a red exclamation mark, make any changes they recommend. If you have the time and resources, aim to fix the yellow ones too. If you are unsure of how to do any of the above yourself, it can be worth hiring an expert to do this for you.

- **Link building**

"A backlink is a hyperlink from a third-party website to yours."[25] These are important as they impact your ranking on Google. Google uses backlinks to measure your site's validity, relevancy, and authority. Focus on getting high-quality back-links from good reputable websites to your webpage.[26] It could be from an article. It could be from YouTube. The more reputable sites that link to yours, the better. You can guest blog or ask partners/distributors/suppliers to mention your website. You can ask for credit from other people who have praised your products. You can get influencers to mention your site, etc. Popular sites are like *Forbes* or *Business Insider*; you would rank highly with backlinks from these places.

- **Keyword research**

Conducting keyword research is an extension of buyer persona research (research on your ideal customer, their pain points, their job, where they spend time online, etc.). You can use the personas to search for the ideal keywords that match your brand and use tools like KW Finder to find related keywords for your target audience.[27]

Content Marketing

Eighteen percent of marketers said that content marketing had the greatest impact on their business[28] ; this may be because content marketing increases audience retention, gives you better social media traction, enhances SEO effort, establishes trust with the audience, improves conversions, and builds authority.[29] Content marketing is where you create and distribute content that has value, is relevant, and is regular to attract and retain your customers and influence them to purchase from you. You should ensure quality, relevance, SEO optimization, optimized for readers, and consistency with what you create. Inbound marketing (creating valuable content and customers finding you) generates three times as many leads as outbound marketing (where you initiate the conversation and send it to an audience) and costs 62% less.[30]

- **Video Marketing**

Videos can be used for landing pages, social media, webinars, emails, and other purposes. On average, businesses create eighteen videos per month; this shows that video is an essential part of your digital marketing strategy.[31] Five key benefits to using videos are that they can improve SEO, keep users on a website for longer, are captivating, convert more customers, and a video is easy to share. [32] Over 50% of consumers like to see videos from brands, perhaps because watching a video requires less effort than reading, it's more visual, it appeals to the senses of sight and sound, and people process and retain what is said in videos more than just text.[33] There are several ways you could create videos to conduct marketing; two key ways are via TikTok or YouTube.

Ninety-two percent of businesses think videos are important to their overall marketing strategy, possibly because statistics support this; users spend 88% more time with video content than any other content. Sixty-six percent of people visit a marketer's site after watching a branded video.[34] There are explainer videos, presentation videos, sales videos, and video ads.[35] You can also get customers to do product review videos via YouTube, and apps like VideoWise will search, verify, and show these reviews on your site.

- **Blogging**

A blog is a regularly updated website or webpage for personal or business use. Businesses that use blogs get 67% more leads than those that do not. Blogs are rated as the fifth most trusted source for accurate online information, which can do wonders to build your reputation as a leader and expert in your field, helping to build credibility.[36] It would be good to create a blog and provide free informative, helpful content to others to share your expertise. You can also do this on panels and forums. Blogging will generate organic traffic for people who haven't decided to purchase yet. It will also show your credibility and build a relationship between your readers and your business over time.[37]

If you don't have time to create the blog content yourself, you could hire a freelancer to create blogs or promotional content for you. Upwork has freelancers who can make blogs and videos or take photos. The more often SEO keywords appear in high-quality and helpful content, the more likely you will appear in search engine results.[38] Your blog could contain commentary on current events, interviews of interesting people, list posts, and reports on trends or events.

- **eBooks & Whitepapers**

An eBook is often an extended guide on a topic for the general audience. In contrast, a whitepaper is more of an academic report on a topic with new research or information for a niche audience of experts.[39] You can repurpose blog posts and other content on your website to create eBooks and whitepapers. The benefits of eBooks and whitepapers are that they show you have expertise in a certain area and provide free content you could exchange for an email address as a customer lead generation tool. Having this free information builds trust and credibility with customers.[40] Depending on the products or services you provide, you could create how-to guides that showcase your skillset, and if customers find this useful, they may buy into more assistance from you.

- **Case Studies & Customer Testimonials**

Ask for customer feedback; this is important for many reasons because you will see if you are providing a solution for customers and meeting their needs, and you'll gauge a sense of customer satisfaction on how you're performing as a business. Also, customers who feel you understand their needs and value their business will return to you, especially if you've remedied any complaints and have resolved them. You can find out customer opinions via surveys to determine what they like about your products/services, their opinion on your competition, and areas for improvement.[41] If customers say they like your products or services, encourage them to share this on Yelp, Google, or social media. Having customer testimonials is one of the most credible sources of information for other prospective customers—so good reviews are a perfect form of marketing.

- **Podcasts**

Five benefits of podcasting for business include that it's
convenient for you and your audience, it helps to build a
connection with your listeners, it helps to build brand authority, it's great to raise brand awareness, and it increases website
traffic.[42] In 2023, there will be 160 million podcast listeners in
the United States. You could start your own podcast or become
a guest on someone else's podcast.[43] Podcasts are a great way to
reach an audience; you don't need to be too technical or invest
much to create one. It is worth being aware that podcasts can
take a while to build traction, so be patient and keep putting
out episodes. Podcasts often want interesting people to inter-
view, so even if you don't want to create your own podcast, you
could share your experience on someone else's existing
podcast.

Affiliate Marketing

Affiliate marketing is where an influencer promotes a product
and gains a commission, or two related businesses help to
market each other.[44] The affiliate generates leads and sales.
Typically, 15% of digital media industry revenue comes from
affiliate marketing.[45] You can develop partnerships with
complementary businesses, products, or services, or start your
own affiliate program; when you partner with another
company, you both benefit. For example, when Altus Mountain
Guides (courses/training for backcountry) partnered with Evo
(an outdoor gear retailer), they had similar customers. If
someone buys something from the store, they get an online

course introduction. If someone books a course, they get a discount code for the Evo store. Suppose you want an affiliate partnership, find someone with a similar audience to you so that you can benefit from one another. You could partner with a trusted comparison site to get your products to the right people.

To grow your affiliate program, you must contact affiliates and influencers to promote your products for a commission. If they sell any products through their site, they could receive a 25% commission on any products bought through their links.[46] However, it is important to establish a brand identity before having an affiliate program because this establishes trust and loyalty, and because your affiliate may engage in discussions across multiple marketing channels, a consistent brand nurtures credibility among new and existing customers.[47]

One technique that affiliates can implement is to create comparison articles, whereby they include your product or service in a list of similar ones by other businesses and weigh up the pros and cons of each one. These articles are great because they showcase your product without being too pushy and let the audience make consumer decisions.

If you're trying to find possible people who could be affiliates, you can use tools like SEMRush to find high-authority websites and SNOV.io to hunt down the contact info of audiences you want to know about your product or service. You could send 3–5 emails to these potential partners. Look at what your competitors offer their affiliates. You could offer free products, incentive bonuses, and higher commissions to gain them as an affiliate. You can set up a contract for affiliates to ensure clear communication and expectations.

Social Media Marketing

- **Organic social media**

Seventy percent of Americans regularly use Facebook, Twitter, and Instagram. The average person spends three hours a day on social media.[48] This makes social media a place to interact with customers, build brand loyalty, and create authentic relationships. You can share news, showcase staff members, highlight any community or non-profit connections, engage with your audience via polls, contests, linking to holiday events, and try retargeting, where a customer looked at your website but didn't follow through with a sale, so retargeting ads on Facebook and Instagram can drive traffic to your website.[49] Other social media platforms for ads include Twitter, LinkedIn, and Instagram (via its Shoppable tool); Pinterest ads have three times the conversion rate of other platforms.[50] You can use social media for customer service and ensure you answer customer questions to ensure your business is responsive and credible. It's worth using location-based hashtags because they allow you as a business to reach people worldwide simply by adding a location tag to a post.

- **Influencer marketing**

Influencers have many followers on social media; they tend to be popular and have built up a reputation for their knowledge and expertise on a specific topic. They tend to be someone in your niche or industry with sway over your target audience. Therefore, they can influence potential product or service buyers by recommending the items on social media. Generally, influencers are popular and liked by their audience. If you were to work with one and ask them to promote your brand, you would pay them to do so, and because of their influence, their followers may start to buy your brand.[51]

- **Facebook ads**

These will help to grow your audience and drive more visitors to your site. Facebook has a very large user base, allowing you to advertise to consumers where they spend much time. There are lots of data behind the scenes, which allows you to target your ads for specific demographics of location, interests, age, sex, online behavior, etc.[52] There is a Facebook Ads Manager that allows you to run and test different ads to try to find a formula that brings lots of customers to you. There is a tool called AdEspresso that can help to run ad campaigns and get good ROI.[53] Facebook ads can have a variety of formats, including single images, videos, and carousels.[54]

- **Leverage user-generated content**

User-generated content (UGC) is content that has been created by someone not officially connected to your business. So, this could be a social media update, a review, a video, a podcast, etc. If the content mentions your brand and no one who works for your business has created it, it is user-generated.[55] User-generated content is important because marketers are often seen as untrustworthy—making false claims and promises to gain a sale. Marketers are seen as biased toward showing the product or service in a favorable light. So, if you can encourage customers to share photos and videos about your products, this content has come from real customer experience and is perceived by other prospective customers as more trustworthy.[56] You could run a photo competition or a raffle. Encourage customers to spread the word because word-of-mouth reviews and testimonials go a long way to making your business successful.

Email Marketing

Use marketing automation to send promotion emails, welcome emails, thank you emails, and abandoned cart emails, to remind people of birthdays/anniversaries, plus re-engagement emails to bring back customers who haven't shopped for a while, perhaps with a welcome-back offer or discount.[57] Email marketing is powerful in gaining and retaining customers because emails go directly to the customer, and they can read them at a convenient time. You can personalize the email to ensure that it's relevant and that customers are updated with the latest products and promotions. Seventy-three percent of millennials like business communication to reach them via email. You could experiment with newsletters and use marketing automation software. You could set up a customer relationship management (CRM) system to send your email marketing. There are CRM tools that do not require a big investment, like ActiveCampaign, Mailchimp, and Constant

Contact. And the top player in the market is Salesforce. You can offer coupons in newsletters or on landing pages so that readers get your products/services at a discounted rate. You can segment your mailing list and target your messages appropriately.[58]

In general, the optimal way to start a marketing funnel is with a 'lead magnet,' which you offer in exchange for a website visitor's email address; a lead magnet is something free or a special deal that is offered to customers in exchange for their contact details; it could be a free digital download, a free service trial, site membership, a coupon, a 'seat' at a webinar, etc.[59] The main goal of a lead magnet is to attract a lead. So, to attract a potential customer who will hopefully convert to purchasing your product or service. Emails have the advantage of being low cost, with a worldwide reach, easy to automate and segment, immediate communication, easy to set up and run, and easy to track and optimize. Email marketing for ecommerce stores has an average return of $42 for every dollar spent.[60] There will be 4.3 billion email users by the end of 2023.[61] Having a clear subject line is good to ensure readers open your email.

Pay-Per-Click Marketing

Pay-per-click marketing (PPC) will drive users to your website while you wait for SEO implementation.[62] There are PPC programs like Google AdWords or Microsoft Advertising that help customers find your business. Your landing page wants to be as optimized as possible before using PPC because if you're paying per click, you want those clicks to convert to sales, so you don't waste your money.[63] PPC ads can boost brand awareness by 80%, and figures show that you usually double what you spend on ads in revenue.[64] With PPC, you can set flexible, affordable budgets as low as $5 and pay only when someone clicks on your ad. You can target customers based on their behavior and past actions.[65]

- **Google Ads**

Because organic traffic takes a while to build up, as a small business, you sometimes need a boost and will want to have a short-term tactic. Google Ads are ideal if you know that your target audience is searching the web for your product or service.[66] If you don't think your target audience is searching the internet, you may want to use social media ads instead. Setting up Google Ads can be slightly tricky, but you can reach a large target market, run retargeting campaigns, and drive more traffic and sales.

Mobile Marketing

The majority of Google searches are carried out on mobiles. Your site needs to look clean and be easy to move through. Google rewards people who have a mobile site by putting your website higher up in the rankings. Many platforms offer mobile-optimized templates.

- **SMS Marketing**

Ensure you have a smooth mobile transaction process, where everything displays correctly and is just as easy to navigate via mobile as a laptop. Ninety percent of texts are opened and read, compared to 20–30% of emails. Texts are cheap to send and a great way to connect with customers.[67] To get a subscriber list, you can get SMS service providers and add opt-in forms to your website and social media profiles.

Online Reputation Management

- **Ratings and Reviews**

Seventy-five percent of shoppers use reviews to help them decide whether to purchase a product.[68] You can ensure that whenever a customer buys a product, an automated email asks them to review the product or experience. You could also encourage referrals and endorsements by offering discounts and deals to existing customers who refer your business to their friends and family.[69] Referrals drive more than $6 trillion of annual consumer spending; a referred customer is 18% more loyal than those who haven't been referred to and tend to spend 13% more on purchases.[70] Eighty-four percent of people trust online reviews as much as they would a friend's recommendation, so it's worth asking customers to leave reviews. Please respond to all reviews and make it easy for customers to leave reviews; if there are any negative reviews, be sure to resolve them and turn them into positive ones.[71]

The top four things to implement are setting up good SEO, email marketing, video marketing, and gaining ratings and reviews. Over time you can add other aspects longer term.

Chapter Checklist:

1. Review the digital marketing strategies above and find at least two that work best for your business idea.
2. Spend as much time as you need following the steps above to formulate your business plan.

The key takeaways from the chapter include the following:

1. Test different digital marketing strategies to find what works for you.
2. Having a documented marketing plan is more likely to lead to success.
3. When creating a marketing plan: assess your current business; set a financial/time budget; outline marketing goals using SMART goals; identify the target audience; determine marketing tactics; and prioritize your tasks.
4. There are many different types of digital marketing strategies. SEO; optimize and localize website; update title tags and meta descriptions; get quality backlinks; use keyword research; do various content marketing (blogs, videos, eBooks, whitepapers, case studies, testimonials, and podcasts). Use affiliate marketing and social media marketing. Use influencers. You can have Facebook ads; user-generated content; email marketing; pay-per-click (PPC); Google Ads; mobile

marketing; SMS; online reputation management with ratings and reviews; and local search marketing using Google My Business.

A marketing strategy is important and links nicely to the next chapter about writing a business plan.

8

PUTTING IT ALL TOGETHER: HOW TO WRITE A WINNING BUSINESS PLAN

"Plan for what is difficult while it is easy; do what is great while it is small."

— SUN TZU

We've been exactly where you are now, with a great business idea and hesitation about formulating that on paper into an official business plan. A white piece of paper has never been more intimidating.

If you're super busy trying to start a new business, part of you may wonder if you have the time to sit down and formulate a business plan. I can assure you, you do, and it's worthwhile to spend time doing, which will assure you success. It's not a fruitless tick-box exercise. It will get things fixed in your head, on calendars with goals to work for that have deadlines; you'll have a sound idea about how every aspect of your business will run and areas where you need to seek expertise or upskill swiftly. Your business plan pushes you to act like nothing else will do. It's the ins and outs, the nitty-gritty of your business, which is best to thoroughly research now rather than too late when you're in the middle.

If you're at a loss as to where to start with writing one, in this chapter, we want to break down a business plan into easy bite-sized chunks so that you can get a good draft version and build upon this.

This chapter will walk you through writing a business plan step-by-step. Having the best intentions and dreams is fine, but this is just a starting point. What you need to do is to put your intentions into action via a business plan. You should stick to it if you focus on the necessary steps to ensure your business ideas succeed.

Peter F. Drucker, an Austrian-American management consultant known as the father of management thinking, stated: "Unless commitment is made, there are only promises and hopes, but no plans."[1] The idea is that if you don't have a fixed plan, you're just making a wish that something will happen. This is crucial and can help you make good business decisions and prevent you from squandering time away by asking yourself about your activities, 'How will this help my future self?' So, this leads us to why you need a business plan.

WHY YOU NEED A BUSINESS PLAN

When you start a business, you'll be pulled in many directions and expected to wear different hats: admin, finance, tax, compliance, HR, marketing, social media manager, sales, IT expert, etc. Without a clear business plan, it's easy to lose track of where you're headed. Seventy percent of business owners do recommend writing a business plan before starting.[2] The key quote is: 'Fail to plan, plan to fail.' Having a solid business plan can tell you if it's viable to give up your 9–5 job to start your business and improves the chances of business success, giving you a clear road map for growth and development. It ensures you know who you are, what you plan to do, and how you will achieve that. Businesses with a business plan grow 30% faster than businesses without, and according to the Harvard Business Review, entrepreneurs with business plans are 16% more likely to build a successful company.[3] Owners with a business plan are twice as likely to get investment compared to those who don't. And when you have a business plan, you are 260% more likely to grow your business from an 'idea' to a 'new business' with a plan.[4]

When you put together a plan, it can also highlight any 'unknowns' or 'gaps' in the business that you may not have thought about otherwise, which may prompt you to ask for help, delegate the task, or even upskill yourself.[5] The three key reasons you need a business plan include the following:

1. Strategic Planning
2. Partnerships
3. Funding Requests

We'll take a closer look at these in turn:

1. Strategic Planning

You must explain why you are in business and why people should choose you. What do you offer, and what are your advantages? What problems do you solve for people? Be clear about who the major players are who shape the business goals. Clarify your ideas, understand the scope of your business, and be clear about how much time, money, and resources you need to achieve this.

2. Partnerships

When you have a clear business plan, it's easier to attract people who may want to form partnerships with you. It's much easier for them to read through your business plan and determine whether they think they'd be a good match.

3. Funding Requests

Again, having a nice clear business plan is attractive to potential investors. It shows that you have thoroughly researched your business idea, thought ahead to the future, and have seriously thought about your competition, your edge, and what you expect to achieve in profits.

Is there a demand for your product or service? Do you have a solid team in place to support your goals? Can you scale the business? It will help the investor determine whether it is a sensible and viable investment; they don't want to lose money. Most venture capitalists and all banks will not invest in a small business without a solid plan.[6]

HOW TO WRITE A BUSINESS PLAN

In America, the United States Small Business Administration (SBA) has a 'write your business plan page' with some sample business plans to download, a template, and a step-by-step plan tool.[7] If you're in a different country, look for an official administration or service that provides relevant information by searching for your country's government business services, state/province, or city government business services. Some Chamber of Commerce websites will offer guides too. You could also look for business plan guides/samples and templates followed by the names of the largest banks in your area.[8] The Bplans website also has over 500 free sample business plans categorized according to different industries. These steps are in order of importance, not necessarily the order in which the sections should be organized in your plan.

Step 1: Describe Your Business

Include a mission statement, history, and objectives. Your mission statement is why your business exists; it should make others believe in your vision and connect with your audience emotionally. What motivates you? What cause/experience led you to start the business, what problem will you solve, and what wider social issues are you passionate about? When describing the company's history, write its founding date, major milestones, location, number of employees, and leadership roles, and mention any flagship products or services.

Your business objectives should be SMART goals that are time-bound and can be measured, i.e., things like 'over the next three years to complete X projects per year (that increase incrementally over the three years); increase revenue from XXX to XXX,' etc. If you have a website domain name, include this here.[9]

Step 2: Talk about Your Product or Service

What unique features does your product or service have? How can you show these are benefits to the customer? Ensure you have intellectual property rights or any patents that protect differentiation. Be clear about how you create your product or service, where you source materials, how they're assembled, how you maintain quality control, how they'll be received or delivered (supply chain), and how you'll manage bookkeeping/inventory. If your product has a life cycle, be aware of the time between purchases, upsells, cross-sells, and downsells, and your plans for research and development.

Step 3: Marketing and Sales Plan

Summarize market research and potential, knowing your target market demographics of location, income, age, gender, education, profession, and hobbies. You need to demonstrate that your target market is specific. Show again your value proposition, ideal target markets, existing customer segments, your plan to attract new business, growth tactics to expand, retention strategies like loyalty or referral programs, advertising and promotion channels, like search engines, social media, videos, etc.[10] How will you reach the market? Through a website or trade shows, or paid advertising?[11] Think about the 4 Ps of marketing: Price, Produce, Promotion, and Place. Why have you chosen the price for the product or service? What are you selling regarding the product, and how will you differentiate it? Promotion is about getting your products in front of your customers. And Place is where you'll sell your products. For online marketing, create a digital content strategy where you create and produce articles and videos, etc.

Step 4: Detail Out Your Logistics and Operations

These are the workflows to make things happen. Your logistics and operations will differ depending on whether you sell products or a service. You may need to consider where you get the raw materials for production if you sell products. Do you make, manufacture, wholesale, or dropship products? How long does it take to produce and get them shipped to you? Can you handle a busy season or an unexpected spike in demand for both product and service businesses? Where will you work from? Do you need a physical space? What equipment, tools, and technology do you need; this includes computers, lightbulbs, stationery, etc. Will you fulfill orders yourself or use a third-party fulfillment partner? How much inventory will you have, where will you store it, and how will you ship it to partners if this is needed?[12] If you're providing a service, is this in person or online? What technology will you need to assist you in doing this? Are there other members of staff remotely who you'll need to communicate and work with to provide your service? Consider the logistics and operations of this.

Step 5: Financial Plan and Projections

Your business needs to be financially viable to survive. If your business is already established, include statements, balance sheets, etc., for the past 3–5 years.

- **Cash Flow Statement**

Have an income statement/cash flow statement. This should show your monthly projected revenue and expenses. Essentially this should easily show your profit or loss during this time. A cash flow differs slightly from the income statement because it shows when revenues are collected and expenses are paid.[13] This is a positive cash flow if you have more income coming in than cash going out. If the opposite is the case, your cash flow is negative.

- **Break Even Analysis**

Have profit and loss statements. This should show how many sales you need to make to cover your initial expenses.

- **Balance Sheet**

Have a balance sheet. This should show your business's current assets (what you own), liabilities (what you owe), and equity (this is the assets minus the liabilities).

Have info on how much revenue you retain as income, your ratio of liquidity to debt repayment, and how often you collect on your invoices. Have three years' worth of reporting and ensure figures are accurate. Avoid underestimating business costs; think about all your overheads. Business insurance premiums tend to increase each year.

Step 6: Investment Needs

Outline the amount of money your business needs and be realistic with your figures. You may need to sell 'equity,' a portion of your company, to raise capital. An equity owner may want to make some decisions in the business, so be careful about who you let fund/invest in your business. The investor may also want dividends (a share of the company profits), and you'll need a clear idea of how they can sell their ownership interest. You'll need to repay any creditors, plus interest on the debt. Try to ensure you have timelines for investors so that they know what to expect. Investors will want to know what their return on investment is likely to be. Some investors want a hands-on role, while others won't want to be involved in day-to-day activities. All investors will want to know when they can get their money back and at what rate.[14] It's sensible to be able to explain how much funding you'll need over five years and what you'll use it for. State whether the funds will be used to buy equipment, and materials, pay salaries, cover bills, etc.

Step 7: Discuss Market Analysis and Competition Research Findings

You could break the market analysis into three: audience analysis, industry analysis, and competitive analysis. Identify your competitors, then know where they advertise, what press coverage they get, how good their customer service is, their sales and pricing strategies, and how they rank on third-party platforms. What sets your business apart from theirs?[15] Show you know the market and that there is a demand for your product or service.[16] How big is it? Have an ideal customer profile. Research industry trends and trajectories. Can you offer lower prices than competitors? Are you distinct from competitors? Do you have a niche segment of the market?

Step 8: Describe Ownership, Management, and Personnel

This is about how you'll staff and manage your business. Outline the legal structure of your business—what type of business is it? Is it a C or S corporation, a limited partnership, a sole proprietor, or a limited liability company (LLC)? You could include an organizational chart to show structure, roles, responsibilities, and relationships. Write one paragraph about each team member, including yourself. List founders and officers and their contributions (both capital and expertise) to the company.[17]

- **Business structure**

Identify who are the CEO, managers, bookkeeper, attorney, staff, etc. List their professional background, awards, and honors.

- **Your team and key people**

Identify your team and know their strengths of how they can make your business a success or grow it. Be clear about their expertise and qualifications.

Step 9: Write Your Business Plan – Executive Summary

- **How to write an executive summary**

The executive summary will set out your business's value proposition or unique selling point. Who is it for (target customers), and what are they dissatisfied with (current solutions)? What does your product or service solve (customer problems)? Use these pointers as a starting point. It should cover the business concept, goals and vision, description and differentiation, target market, marketing strategy, current financial state, projected financial state, the ask (if you're asking for money), and the team.[18]

- **This should be last since it is a summary of your plan**

While this will form the very first part of your plan, it should be written last. You can condense the key ideas from the other sections of your plan. It should be short, usually one page or less, and give an overview of your business. For people who are short on time and want to get the idea of your business swiftly, this is the purpose of your executive summary.[19]

Step 10: Have an Appendix of Official Documents

Having an appendix of official documents shows that your business plan is well-organized and meticulous. Your investors can use it to do due diligence. If your business plan is shared with employees, they have context and easy access to everything they need. You can include deeds, permits, legal documents, certifications, business registries and licenses, patents, associations/memberships, state ID numbers, key customer contracts, and purchase orders. You could also include testimonials, research excerpts, charts, and other information relevant to your business. You could put credit histories, resumes, product brochures, permits, and supplier contracts in your appendix.[20]

TIPS FOR CREATING YOUR BUSINESS PLAN

- **Know your audience**

Who will be reading your plan—tailor the language to them and include the most relevant information and figures. Omit sections that aren't as relevant to them.[21]

- **Have a clear goal**

If you're trying to secure funding, you must deliver a more thorough plan.

- **Invest time in research**

Know your margins and be clear about every cost your business incurs. Do research from independent sources. Know who you're selling to and the demand and be aware of competitors.

- **Keep a realistic timeline**

If it takes most companies 6–12 months to get up and running, this is how long it will take you. Always give yourself more time than you think it will take. So, if you expect it to be three months, give yourself six months to allow for unseen delays.[22]

- **Keep it short and to the point**

Around 10–20 pages should be sufficient. Put any other important documents in the appendix.

- **Keep the tone, style, and voice consistent**

Make it easy to read, with nice clear sections. Try to have just one person writing the plan and edit it thoroughly before the final version.

- **Conduct a SWOT analysis**

Before starting your business, conducting a SWOT analysis, and considering your business's strengths, weaknesses, opportunities, and threats is a good idea. What do you think your company will do well? What do you think you will struggle with? Are there any changes that you could take as an opportunity? Are there any threats that could mean you're not able to succeed? Strengths and weaknesses are internal, whereas opportunities and threats are external. This analysis allows businesses to see their current situation and plan for the future.[23] It gives your business a focus on goals, allows you to see the bigger picture, improves communication and collaboration, and helps you to gain insight and make informed decisions. To conduct a SWOT analysis, draw a cross on a piece of paper, and in each of the four segments, consider the strengths, weaknesses, opportunities, and threats.

- **Write using the 'BLUF' format (bottom line up front)**

A BLUF approach (bottom line up front) is where the key information is placed right at the start of the text rather than the end. It develops credibility, and readers think the writing is crisp and confident, that of an expert. It works a bit like an elevator speech. It lets readers get the gist even if they haven't read the entire document. It can also guide readers through the journey, so they know the most important bits. Covering who, what, where, when, and why is often useful. There is the acronym BLIND too, which can cover Bottom Line, its Impact on the organization, the Next steps to be taken, and Details.[24]

Chapter Checklist:

1. Get a notepad and pen or open a Word document (or equivalent) and have a go at writing the ten parts of a business plan.
2. You can also find templates for a business plan online or via the Consulting Club.
3. Use spell-check or Grammarly to check your plan for errors; get a few friends/family to proofread it too. You want it to look professional. Make sure to give yourself plenty of time to polish your business plan.

The key takeaways from this chapter are:

1. Be committed to creating/writing a plan, act upon it, and follow it through.
2. A business plan will help your business to grow 30% more than people who don't have one; you'll be 260% more likely to move from an idea to a new business and 16% more likely to be successful.
3. A business plan will help with strategy, partnerships, and funding.
4. Ten steps to creating a business plan include: 1. Describe your business. 2. Talk about your product or service. 3. Have a marketing and sales plan. 4. Detail logistics and operations. 5. Financially plan and have projections. 6. Think about investment needs. 7. Do a market analysis and know your competition. 8. Write in detail about your ownership, management, and

personnel. 9. Write an executive summary. 10. Have appendices of supporting documents.

5. Tailor the language to the audience. Do thorough research. Keep it realistic and brief. Be consistent. Do a SWOT analysis. Use BLUF writing.

Now that you know how to create a solid business plan, you can start implementing your dreams. The next and final chapter looks at the secrets to entrepreneurial success and how to overcome obstacles.

9

PAVING THE ROAD TO SUCCESS

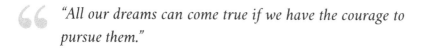 *"All our dreams can come true if we have the courage to pursue them."*

— **WALT DISNEY**

This chapter will inspire and motivate you to act in the face of adversity. The path to running a successful business isn't always smooth. Most businesses face some challenges; within the chapter, you will see various success stories that show how other digital entrepreneurs have overcome seemingly insurmountable challenges and have managed to turn their businesses into success. It is important to acknowledge that, according to *Entrepreneur*, many people experience a lack of confidence that prevents them from pursuing their dreams or making important changes to their business. Another thing that can get in the way of success is a lack of motivation and a feeling of being lazy.[1] Never give up on your business dreams;

find a way to make them happen. You may see some other small businesses that had challenges and see that they overcame them. If they can, so can you! By the end of this chapter, you will know 'the recipe' that helped many small businesses overcome challenges like failure, uncertainty, lack of money, the loneliness of a solopreneur, and the risks of scaling and hiring staff; you may resonate with some of these. There are some hints and tips on how to try to alleviate these fears and still go ahead and run your business anyhow! Sometimes, research, preparation, finding information, and being as prepared as possible will help.

AGAINST ALL ODDS: SUCCESS STORIES OF SMALL BUSINESS

Many businesses have encountered challenges and have managed to overcome them. Below you will find some stories of these to inspire you and to help you know that even when you face challenges, there are ways around them.

Spanish to Move

Luis Pelayo created the business Spanish to Move, where he and his team would teach Spanish in fun and easy-to-understand online courses. He has differentiated his product to make it stand out from competitors. Luis initially worked a separate job and was running his business in parallel. He found it challenging because he couldn't dedicate 100% to the online course business; he emphasized developing patience. One key challenge was that as they grew their online course business, they found it hard to keep track of different elements. They needed to pay professionals to help in different areas like web page design and marketing. They decided to move their business to the platform Thinkific to host their courses. Because the platform came with experts, it was easy for them to adapt web pages without needing to pay for a web designer or have programming knowledge. He was able to integrate his email list and marketing tools, so everything is under one platform, making it more manageable for him. They've taken advantage of all integrations regarding how customers pay to keep everything neatly on one platform. This worked well; they enrolled seventy new students in their course in the first month! Louis said that another key challenge was managing his time, especially when working in his regular job most of the day. His advice for how to do that is to work consistently every day and to minimize distractions to be consistent, disciplined, and persistent.[2]

Phones International Group

Peter Jones, who is now one of the 'Dragons' on the show *Dragon's Den* founded a computer company when he was in his twenties; it had some success but then collapsed, and as a result, he had to give up his home and possessions. He took a job at Siemens and got back on his feet. He later invested £1,000 to set up Phones International Group, a wireless communications company that became one of Europe's fastest-growing businesses. The key takeaway from this is that even successful people and businesses may have faced financial hardship and experienced risk and failure in the past. Still, with a true entrepreneurial mindset, they learn from it and keep persevering until they are successful.

Night Owl Cleaning Services

The key takeaway of the success story that will follow is that regardless of your background, if you have a great business idea and can fill a niche in the market, you can create a successful business. Arlete Turturro founded Night Owl Cleaning Services; while she has qualifications in fashion and real estate, she now runs a commercial cleaning company that also provides party attendants and 24-hour emergency services. This shows that you can start on one or two different pathways and end up in a different place. It's about seeing and filling a need, and being flexible, which can often lead to wonderful things. Some people may be dismissive of people who hold cleaning jobs, but cleaning homes and offices at weekends could lead to greater things like running a major successful business![3]

GooRoo

The key takeaway in this challenge is that even in what seems like a broad market segment, it is possible to find a niche and differentiate yourself. GooRoo, a learning platform, was founded by Scott Lee, who believes everyone deserves a good education and set up a platform to connect students to the perfect tutor. It has over 1,000 tutors in New York and trains more tutors nationwide. Scott's problem was that, as a small business, how he could tackle something as large as education.

He believes everyone has individual needs, which is how his platform helps.[4] His challenge was finding a niche in such a large topic. Still, he made a successful business by focusing on individuality, embracing diversity, and matching tutors to specific learning needs. Lee founded a company when he was in high school. After that, he served in the army, founded another company, worked for JPMorgan, and was an advisor for the 2018 Olympics; after all that, he founded GooRoo. He drew upon a diverse experience set to help him run the best business and become a better CEO. [5]

DC Mosquito Squad

Damian Sanchez founded DC Mosquito Squad. It's a pest control business. His challenge was struggling to keep track of all his leads in Washington, D.C. His solution was to invest in software to automate sales and marketing opportunities. This helped him onboard new team members, renew customers with just an email address, and scale his business.[6]

THE TOP 5 FEARS FOR BUSINESS OWNERS AND HOW TO OVERCOME THEM

1. Fear of Failure

Thirty-nine percent of new business owners give fear of failure as their main concern.[7] However, you can turn the fear of failure into a learning opportunity to apply lessons learned and not run from it but help spur you on. Starting a new business can be scary, and you may worry about failure; that's a natural concern. It's important to weigh up the risks and do your market research to ensure that you have a viable business idea.

There is the oft-repeated but worthwhile quote from Thomas Edison, who stated: 'I have not failed. I've just found 10,000 ways that won't work.' This is a true positive testament to if, at first, you don't succeed, try, try, and try again, and learn each time from this so that you can make improvements to previous attempts. Have a growth mindset as an entrepreneur where you don't view mistakes as failures but as an opportunity to learn. You need to adapt and evolve. Vanessa Molica, who owns The Lash Professional, says that she never gives in to her fear of failure because she has "too much to do and too many goals to achieve to let this kind of fear paralyze me. Rather than let it rule me, I use my fear of failure as fuel for my continued success."[8]

2. Wrestling with Uncertainty

Thirty-one percent of business owners are concerned about doing something wrong.[9] When you don't know the right option, this can sometimes feel paralyzing. You will likely have days when you wrestle with uncertainty and wonder if you have done the right thing by starting your business when things go wrong, or business is slow. A good solution can be to gather as much information as possible before you make an important decision, look at the outcome of your actions, and move forward.[10]

But, there's a quote that Lynda Houston, owner of Salvage & Bloom employs at such times to give her motivation, and this is: Remember Why You Started. You won't have entered the business without a passion and reason for doing it; on tough days, remind yourself of what motivated you. That is still worth fighting for! John A. Shedd states: 'A ship in the harbor is safe, but that is not what ships are built for.' So this means that you will need to push yourself outside of your comfort zone, take some risks, and not always stay where you know it is safe and secure to achieve all you are meant to in life.

3. Not Having Enough Money/Funding

Eighty percent of companies with less than 500 employees make it through their first year. Seventy percent are operating at the end of the second year, and only 50% make it to five years. Almost half of the businesses that shut down do so due to a lack of funds. Don't be daunted by these figures because, in 2018 in the US, 30.2 million small businesses were running . . . which shows it can be done! Financial challenges for businesses can include a limited or inconsistent cash flow, not using a budget, not preparing for unforeseen expenses, not raising enough capital, having too much debt, not doing financial reporting/taxes, not paying bills on time, mixing business and personal finances, and poor marketing.[11] You can offer customers discounted payments if they pay quickly, send through timely invoices with proactive reminders, prioritize customers with large balances in the collection process, and have weekly financial targets.

Try to look at historical performance and current conditions, think about economic downturns and customer shifts, and do scenario planning to prepare you well. It's good to develop and stick to a living document budget to plan for the future. Having a 'rainy day fund' of cash makes good sense to see you through unforeseen expenses. Knowing your business credit scores and raising enough capital is important if you apply for funding. It would help if you had the capital to hire staff, expand into additional markets, and explore new opportunities.

Many entrepreneurs bootstrap their way to success and take on some business debt. But be cautious that you don't overstretch credit cards or take on a line of credit with too high an interest rate. Look for places where you can reduce costs, and consider creative financing options (angel investors, crowdfunding). If you are struggling financially, contact creditors, let them know your situation, and work with them to help you. Try consolidating business loans into one payment. Remember to keep accurate financial records and file tax forms on time. It would be best to assume all accounts could be audited anytime.

Use well-trusted sources like the US Small Business Administration (SBA) for resources, guides, articles, webinars, etc. Over half of all companies do their accounts payable manually. Still, automated systems can save money and time in the long run, so this could be worth considering as your company grows.[12] Having a separate business and personal bank account helps to manage company inflow and outflow. You need good marketing to ensure a steady flow of new customers.

4. The Loneliness of Being a Solopreneur

This is a common challenge for anyone starting a business. You don't have someone to bounce ideas off, brainstorm with, or ask for advice if things don't work out quite as you'd hoped. There are things you can do to help with this, though; you can join communities to connect with like-minded solopreneurs. If you feel you have a connection to people within those communities, reach out to them to make time for a coffee and a chat or a Zoom call, and stay in touch with them. You could also organize coworking events with other solopreneurs.

5. Risks of Scaling and Hiring Staff

Another quote by Roy Ash is: 'An entrepreneur tends to bite off a little more than he can chew, hoping he'll quickly learn how to chew it.' Any changes you make to your business may be a bit of a step into the unknown, and you may worry about whether you can scale up or hire staff. But you've got this. You can do this! Sometimes you'll learn as you go along. You may not know exactly what you're doing, but you'll figure it out. When you increase your business, you will need more staff to help with the increased workload; this has overheads, and you'll need to trust new people. They will help you to expand, you need to ensure you have the infrastructure to handle exports, and you need to ensure financial and logistical documents are ready to be used.[13]

Chapter Checklist:

1. Spend some time listing and addressing your fears about starting your own business.
2. Develop potential solutions for situations where your worst fears come true.
3. Do you feel you have your business finances sorted? What could you do to improve these?
4. Would you like a support network around you? If so, what could you do to achieve this?
5. Do you wish to expand internationally? Which country will you target first? Do you or a staff member speak the language? Is there competition? Could you form partnerships and build relationships?

Key takeaways from the chapter:

Some of the key takeaways from this chapter include the following:

1. Remember, you can change tack, and it's OK to do that. Be flexible and seize opportunities.
2. It's OK to do different things, sometimes career-wise, before getting to the business you want to run. You can draw upon all prior knowledge and experience; it will always be useful.
3. If you can find a hard-to-get authentic product and make it available to people, this can be profitable. Also,

use social media to keep your customers updated, like TikTok and Pinterest, etc.

4. It can be a good technique to create an experience for customers rather than the brand. Also, aim to get user-generated content from fans.

5. If you find keeping track of leads challenging, you could use some software to automate sales and marketing.

6. If you're concerned about scaling or hiring staff, learn as you go along and figure it out. It would help if you considered language and cultural barriers for international expansion. Learn lessons from experience. Have a member of staff who can speak the local language. Build relationships with local businesses.

7. If you feel lonely, join communities, connect with people for coffee or via Zoom, and organize coworking events.

8. Do thorough research if concerned about failure. Be prepared to try different things to get something to work. Remember, you have many goals to achieve, so get stuck in there and get on with it.

9. If you feel uncertain, again gather all the information you can; then monitor the outcome of the decision and move forward. Remember *why* you started the business to remind you of your passion. You need to push yourself outside of your comfort zone.

10. To overcome money/funding issues, you could offer customers a discount for timely payments, have financial targets, have a living document budget to plan for the future, and have a rainy day fund for unforeseen

costs. Be careful not to incur too much debt. Be upfront with creditors if financially struggling and work with them to find solutions. Consider automated systems to help with financial tasks. Have a separate business account from your personal account. Have good marketing to ensure the flow of customers.

CONCLUSION

We have looked at a lot of different topics over the chapters. But everything goes back to the first point: you need to have an entrepreneurial spirit which means you need to be adaptable, self-reliant, able to solve problems/come up with solutions, and comfortable with risk. Don't fear failure; instead, learn from it. Be independent, responsible, and self-accountable, and make SMART goals. Keep growing, learning, and forward-thinking, and take a long-term perspective. Be aware of your strengths and weaknesses. After examining what it means to have an entrepreneurial mindset, other chapters have explored trends, niches, positioning, pricing, branding, marketing, business plans, and motivation/inspiration.

We have taken you through the steps so that you are not alone but have someone there to advise you. There are numerous reasons why you may have decided to become an entrepreneur; everyone's reasons are unique to them. We at the Consulting

Club have experienced success and have helped startups in healthcare and tech, and we want to help you in your endeavors too. We want to help you have financial freedom and help you to use your skills to make the world a better place.

Here are the chapters covered in the book in a nutshell:

I'm sure you remember that Chapter 1 focused on developing an entrepreneurial mindset before starting to write a business plan which included developing the characteristics and the path to success and embracing failure. We wanted you to develop these entrepreneurial characteristics so that your business succeeds, and you survive as a business owner. Some of the key takeaways from the chapter are that running a successful online business is possible! You need to build an entrepreneurial mindset, find and position your service/product, and build a successful brand. Finally, don't fear failure but learn from it.

In Chapter 2, you may recall we discussed various digital business trends, how to determine whether these were rising or a fad, and how to find niche topics. We want you to be aware of trends and how you could capitalize on them and apply relevant ones to your business to improve the success of your business. Finding the trends can really inform how you operate your business to get the maximum benefit from the trends. One of the key takeaways from the chapter is that many free tools are available to track trends.

If you think back to Chapter 3 of the book, it covered how to find your niche, a unique specialist segment of the market. We wanted to convey that many different tools can help you find a niche and narrow your specific market so that you have an area of expertise that fits your passion and market demand. Again, a key takeaway is that many free tools can help you find your niche.

Chapter 4 of the book examined brand positioning and where your business stands in relation to competitors. We wrote the chapter so you can differentiate your business with a USP and know your customer's perception of your brand and ensure that you serve them. A key takeaway from the chapter is that you can easily conduct perceptual mapping to position your brand in relation to others.

Chapter 5, I'm sure you remember, was about pricing and working out how much you should charge. We wrote the chapter because this is a common issue entrepreneurs struggle with. We discussed the importance of conducting thorough market research and covered various pricing models you could apply to best suit your business and avoid any negative consequences. The chapter gave some pricing strategy examples with existing businesses, so you could see how they worked for them. A key takeaway from the chapter is to re-evaluate your pricing strategy regularly.

You may recall that the topic of branding was looked at in Chapter 6. We wrote the chapter because branding can help create an identity for your business and win customer favorability. The chapter also discussed the twelve archetypes to help build an emotional connection with your audience. Which archetype do you think your business resonates with the most? Raising awareness of your brand, and having customers resonate with your brand is important so that customers purchase your service/products and return to you time and time again. A key takeaway from the chapter is to think about voice, design, values, story, and vibe and pick an archetype.

The final of the seven steps, in Chapter 7, was about marketing. We wrote the chapter as many businesses fail to do all they can to market their business well, and this can be make or break for a business. The chapter covered different marketing strategies and discussed creating a documented marketing plan. Many different marketing techniques and tools were discussed, and it's up to you to apply the ones you think are best suited to your business and experiment with them. A key takeaway from the chapter is to try different digital marketing strategies and check metrics to see which are successful for you.

Chapter 8, I'm sure you remember, was about pulling all the previous chapters' information together to create a solid business plan. We wrote this chapter because we don't want you to just read or listen to a book. We want you to act and put into practice the seven steps and create your online business. The chapter provides clear guidance on the sections you should include in a business plan and tips on the writing/style of it. A key takeaway from the chapter is to create a detailed business plan with supporting documents.

We wrote Chapter 9, the final chapter, intending to motivate, inspire and offer some advice for when times are challenging running your own business. It contains some information on other small businesses that have overcome challenges, and we're certain you will overcome any obstacles in your way. A key takeaway from the chapter is to be prepared, do research, check finances, use social media, use automation, and put work into marketing to secure future customers. Last but not least, learn from failure.

Now you've reached the end of the book, it is time to (if you haven't done so as you've gone along) put each of the seven steps into action. You may also wish to subscribe to the Consulting Club's newsletter and social media channels for up-to-date tips and advice on entrepreneurship and running an online business.

CONSULTING CLUB

The Consulting Club has gone through these steps and keeps going over them over and over, and this is entrepreneurship, a never-ending journey. At the Consulting Club, we intend to empower others to do the same, stepping out of their comfort zone, turning their passions/dreams into an income, and breaking free from their 9–5 jobs. The main goal behind the Consulting Club is not just to encourage people to reach their financial freedom through entrepreneurship but especially to start following their North Star, to follow the motto: 'Love what you do, and you will never work a day in your life.' If you feel you would benefit from a supportive environment with advice from experts, hints and tips, guidance and mentoring, and a forum of fellow entrepreneurs, then please click the following link to learn more: https://theconsultingclub.com/

So, some key advice at this final stage includes:

1. Set a deadline for you to start your business.
2. Go through each of the steps outlined in this book to find your business niche and plan your strategy.

We'd be very grateful if you would please take the time to leave a review and feedback on Amazon so that other people interested in entrepreneurship can find and benefit from this book.

We here at the Consulting Club believe in you! We're proud of you for deciding to become an entrepreneur. You've got this. You can make your business a success and remember that a journey well begun is already half done! We wish you good luck on your online business journey!

We would love to hear about your journey, if you would like to share it with us, please send us an email to Matthew@ theconsultingclub.com

NOTES

INTRODUCTION

1. Startups, 2021.
2. Startups, 2021.
3. My Free Marketing, 2022.
4. Forbes, n.d.
5. Bloomberg reporting, Bloomberg Billionaires Index, n.d.
6. Levy, n.d.
7. Levy, n.d.
8. Jobs, n.d.
9. Tikkanen, n.d.

1. DEVELOPING AN ENTREPRENEURIAL MINDSET

1. Gabrielle, 2021.
2. Todorov, 2022.
3. Failory, 2022.
4. NWIBIZHUB, n.d.
5. NFTE, n.d.
6. Jaskiewicz & Combs, 2017.
7. Cider, 2018.
8. Nevogt, 2022.
9. Nevogt, 2022.
10. Perell, 2020.
11. Business Know-How, 2022.
12. Perell, 2020.
13. Perell, 2020.
14. Brook, 2022.
15. Conlin, n.d.
16. Systeme, n.d.

2. THE TREND IS YOUR FRIEND

1. BigCommerce, n.d.
2. Conlin, n.d.
3. BigCommerce, n.d.
4. Bezzant, 2021.
5. Conlin, n.d.
6. BigCommerce, n.d.
7. Conlin, n.d.
8. Oberlo, n.d.
9. Ferreira, 2020.
10. Ferreira, 2020.
11. Ferreira, 2020.
12. Ferreira, 2020.
13. Ferreira, 2020.
14. Ferreira, 2020.
15. Oberlo, n.d.
16. Ferreira, 2020.
17. Ferreira, 2020.
18. SBA, n.d.
19. Keenan, 2022.
20. Bhat, 2023.
21. SBA, n.d.

3. HOW TO FIND YOUR NICHE

1. Statista, 2022.
2. Sheehan, n.d.
3. Indeed, n.d.
4. Sheehan, n.d.
5. Novak, 2019.
6. Wooll, 2022.
7. Rampton, 2017.
8. Novak, 2019.
9. Junttila, Henri, n.d.
10. ThriveThemes, n.d.
11. DeMatas, 2022.

12. ThriveThemes, n.d.
13. Novak, 2019.
14. Junttila, Henri, n.d.
15. Novak, 2019.
16. DeMatas, 2022.
17. Hart, 2023.
18. Hart, 2023.
19. Novak, 2019.
20. One.com, 2023.
21. Ferreira, 2022.
22. DeMatas, 2022.
23. ThriveThemes, n.d.
24. Decision Link, 2023.
25. Alfred, 2022.
26. ThriveThemes, n.d.
27. Sheehan, n.d.
28. Rampton, 2017.
29. Wooll, 2022.
30. DeMatas, 2022.
31. DeMatas, 2022.
32. DeMatas, 2022.
33. Novak, 2019.
34. Lawrence, 2020.
35. Mandel, 2023.
36. Wooll, 2022.
37. Kamb, 2023.
38. Indeed, n.d.
39. Tanner, 2020.

4. THE POWER OF POSITIONING

1. Spark and Bloom Studio, 2021.
2. Hippos to Horses, 2021.
3. Hart, 2022.
4. Twin, 2022.
5. Heijmans, 2020.are you please able to phone me on my mobile, before coming roX
6. Murphy, 2021.

7. Nachlis, 2020.
8. Shewan, 2014.
9. Hancock, 2022.
10. Shewan, 2014.
11. Shewan, 2014.
12. Shewan, 2014.
13. Hippos to Horses, 2021.
14. Hippos to Horses, 2021.
15. Hart, 2022.
16. Hart, 2022.
17. Heijmans, 2020.
18. Murphy, 2021.
19. Ondreicsik, n.d.
20. Mind Tools Content Team, n.d.
21. Image from: https://conceptboard.com/blog/perceptual-map-template/.
22. Image from: https://conceptboard.com/blog/perceptual-map-template/.
23. Image from: https://conceptboard.com/blog/perceptual-map-template/.
24. Image from: Dinkin, Keren. (2022) How Product Positioning Helps Your Ecommerce Business. *Digital.* Online. https://digital.com/best-ecommerce-platforms/how-product-positioning-helps-your-ecommerce-business/.

5. PRICING YOUR OFFER

1. Yu, Eric, 2022.
2. Decker, Allie, n.d.
3. Odjick, 2022.
4. Mailchimp, 2022.
5. Heaslip, 2023.
6. Freshbooks, 2020.
7. Decker, n.d.
8. Decker, n.d.
9. Decker, n.d.
10. Heaslip, 2023.

6. BRANDING IN A NUTSHELL

1. Jovancic, 2018.
2. Collins, 2022, online.
3. Louise, 2022.
4. Collins, 2022, online
5. Collins, 2022, online
6. Collins, 2022, online
7. Houraghan, 2018.
8. The Hartford. 2023.
9. The Hartford. 2023.
10. Houraghan, 2018.
11. Houraghan, 2018.
12. Louise, 2022.
13. Thomsen, Rikke Berg, 2022.
14. Lehmann, Sascha et al, 2020.
15. Mailchimp, 2022.
16. Mailchimp, 2022.
17. Louise, 2022.
18. Matthew, 2022.

7. LET'S GET MARKETING

1. Keenan, 2022.
2. Heitman, 2022.
3. Heitman, Stephanie, 2022.
4. Small Business Administration, n.d.
5. Heitman, 2022.
6. Mailchimp, 2022.
7. Mailchimp, 2022.
8. Small Business Administration, n.d.
9. Heitman, 2022.
10. Small Business Administration, n.d.
11. Heitman, 2022.
12. Small Business Administration, n.d.
13. Boyarsky, 2022.
14. Daniel, 2022.

15. McCormick, 2020.
16. Keenan, 2022.
17. VWO, 2023.
18. MotionPoint, n.d.
19. Boyarsky, 2022.
20. Uzialko, 2023.
21. Gavril, 2017.
22. Blair, n.d.
23. Uzialko, 2023.
24. Blair, n.d.
25. FatJoe, 2023.
26. McDevitt, 2022.
27. Boyarsky, 2022.
28. Blair, n.d.
29. Designrr, 2022.
30. Keenan, 2022.
31. Turbureanu, 2023.
32. Turbureanu, 2023.
33. Boyarsky, 2022.
34. Turbureanu, 2023.
35. Keenan, 2022.
36. Forsey, 2022.
37. Boyarsky, 2022.
38. McCormick, 2020.
39. Ismail, 2018.
40. McCormick, 2020.
41. Mailchimp, 2022.
42. Buffonmedia, 2022.
43. Keenan, 2022.
44. Howes, 2021.
45. Keenan, 2022.
46. Howes, 2021.
47. Trackdeskblog, 2022.
48. McDevitt, 2022.
49. Mailchimp, 2022.
50. Boyarsky, 2022.
51. Wood, 2021.
52. McCormick, 2020.
53. Blair, n.d.

54. Keenan, 2022.
55. Vrountas, 2023.
56. Mailchimp, 2022.
57. Mailchimp, 2022.
58. McCormick, 2020.
59. Blair, n.d.
60. Keenan, 2022.
61. McDevitt, 2022.
62. Heitman, 2022.
63. Boyarsky, 2022.
64. McCormick, 2020.
65. Keenan, 2022.
66. Boyarsky, 2022.
67. Keenan, 2022.
68. Mailchimp, 2022.
69. Nethercott, 2023.
70. Boyarsky, 2022.
71. McCormick, 2020.

8. PUTTING IT ALL TOGETHER: HOW TO WRITE A WINNING BUSINESS PLAN

1. Michael, 2023.
2. Wahbe, 2023.
3. Hines, 2022.
4. Wahbe, 2023.
5. Odjick, 2022.
6. Wahbe, 2023.
7. Hines, 2022.
8. Hines, 2022.
9. Nexcess, 2022.
10. Wahbe, 2023.
11. Gil, 2021.
12. Odjick, 2022.
13. Odjick, 2022.
14. Entrepreneur, 2015.
15. Wahbe, 2023.
16. Gil, 2021.

17. BigCommerce, 2023.
18. Odjick, 2022.
19. Odjick, 2022.
20. Hines, 2022.
21. Odjick, 2022.
22. Entrepreneur, 2015.
23. Ocasio, 2023.
24. Sridharan, 2023.

9. PAVING THE ROAD TO SUCCESS

1. EWOR Team, 2022.
2. Basu, 2017.
3. Diethelm, 2020.
4. Damien, 2021.
5. Diethelm, 2020.
6. Damien, 2021.
7. Enright, 2021.
8. Farmiloe, 2023.
9. Enright, 2021.
10. Enright, 2021.
11. Beaver, 2020.
12. Beaver, 2020.
13. QuickBooks, 2017.

REFERENCES

Alfred, Lestraundra. (2022). 7 Key Principles of Value-Based Selling. *Hubspot.* Online. 3rd January 2022. https://blog.hubspot.com/sales/value-based-selling.

Ames, Ella. (2021). Digital Marketing Strategies for Small Business. *LiveAbout.* Online. https://www.liveabout.com/top-internet-marketing-strategies-for-the-small-business-2296125.

Augustyn, Adam. (n.d.). Biography of Jeff Bezos. *Encyclopaedia Britannica.* Online. https://www.britannica.com/biography/Jeff-Bezos .

Basu, Tyler. (2017). How to Teach Spanish Online (Case Study). *Thinkific.* Online. https://www.thinkific.com/blog/luis-pelayo-teaches-spanish-lessons-online/ .

Beaver, Scott. (2020). 10 Top Financial Challenges for Small Businesses and How to Overcome Them. *Oracle Netsuite.* September 25th 2020. Online. https://www.netsuite.com/portal/resource/articles/business-strategy/small-business-financial-challenges.shtml.

Bezzant, Bailey. (2021). How to Use Marketing Data to Differentiate Yourselt & Beat Competitors. *Pattern.* Online. 14th January 2021. https://pattern.com/blog/how-to-use-marketing-data-to-differentiate-yourself-and-beat-competitors/.

Bhat, Adi. (2023). Market Research: What it is, Methods, Types & Examples. *QuestionPro.* Online. https://www.questionpro.com/blog/what-is-market-research/.

BigCommerce. (n.d.). E-commerce Trends That Are Powering Online Retail Forward. Online. https://www.bigcommerce.com/articles/ecommerce/ecommerce-trends/.

BigCommerce. (2023). Creating a Stellar Ecommerce Business Plan For Your Online Store. *BigCommerce.* Online. https://www.bigcommerce.com/articles/ecommerce/business-plan/.

Bloomberg Billionaires Index. Jeff Bezos. Online. https://www.bloomberg.com/billionaires/profiles/jeffrey-p-bezos/ .

Boyarsky, Katherine. (2022). 46 Ideas for Your Small Business Marketing Strategy. *HubSpot.* Online. https://blog.hubspot.com/marketing/small-business-marketing-guide.

Brook, Charlotte. (2022). For innovative, risk-taking grads, entrepreneurship is a popular route. If that's you, here are five key ways to develop an entrepreneurial mindset and lead you to success. *Business Because.* Online. https://www.businessbecause.com/news/entrepreneurs/8279/how-to-develop-an-entrepreneurial-mindset?sponsored= .

Browne, Emily. (2022). TikTok Success Stories: 9 Small Businesses That Went Viral. *Shopify*. Online. June 15th 2022. https://www.shopify.com/blog/tiktok-success-stories#6 .

Buffonmedia. (2022). The 5 Benefits of Podcasting for Business. Online. https://www. buffoonmedia.co.uk/podcast-benefits-for-business/ .

BuildFire. (n.d.) 19 Awesome Marketing Strategies for Small Businesses. *BuidFire*. Online. https://buildfire.com/marketing-strategies-for-small-businesses/.

Business Know-How. (2022). How to Develop an Entrepreneurial Mindset. https://www. zenbusiness.com/blog/entrepreneurial-mindset/ .

Business Victoria. (2022). Marketing Action Plan Template. *Business Victoria*. Online. https://business.vic.gov.au/tools-and-templates/marketing-action-plan-template.

Cider, Johanna. (2018). 5 Reasons Why an Entrepreneurial Mindset is Essential for Business. *EMI*. Online. https://engineeringmanagementinstitute.org/entrepreneurial-mindset-essential-business/.

Collins, Alexa. (2022). What is Brand Strategy? Definition and Guide. *Shopify*. Online. https://www.shopify.com/blog/brand-strategy.

Conlin, Bennett. (n.d.) 10 Tech Trends That Will Influence Your Marketing. *Business News Daily*. Online. https://www.businessnewsdaily.com/8564-future-of-marketing.html.

Consultancy.uk. (2019). Four successful companies that overcame early setbacks. *Consultancy.uk*. Online. https://www.consultancy.uk/news/22249/four-successful-compa nies-that-overcame-early-setbacks.

Curry, David. (2022). Amazon Statistics. Online. https://www.businessofapps.com/data/ amazon-statistics/ .

Damien. (2021). Meet Your Heroes: 12 Small Business Success Stories. *Zyro Blog*. Online. https://zyro.com/blog/successful-small-business-stories/.

Daniel, Harry. (2022). 3 Key reasons SEO should be in your 2022 digital strategy. *Rawnet*. Online. https://www.rawnet.com/insights/3-key-reasons-seo-should-be-your-2022-digi tal-strategy?

Decision Link. (2023). Value Selling: The Ultimate Guide to Value-Based & Value-Added Selling. *Decision Link*. Online. https://www.decisionlink.com/value-sellingultimateguide#:

Decker, Allie. (n.d). The Ultimate Guide to Pricing Strategies. Hubspot.https://blog. hubspot.com/sales/pricing-strategy .

DeMatas, Darren. (2022). How to Find a Niche. *ECommerceceo*. Online. https://www.ecom merceceo.com/how-to-find-niche/ .

Designrr. (2022). 13 Reasons Why Content Marketing is Important and How to Get Started. *Designrr*. Online. https://designrr.io/reasons-why-content-marketing-is-important/?

Diethelm, Lauren. (2020). 13 Business Success Stories and What They Teach Entrepreneurs. *Fundera*. Online. 11th November 2020. https://www.fundera.com/blog/business-success-stories.

Dinh, Anh. (2022) Understand What it Takes to Develop an Entrepreneurial Mindset. https://nasdaqcenter.lehigh.edu/blog/how-you-can-develop-entrepreneurial-mindset-11-critical-attributes.

Dinkin, Keren. (2022) How Product Positioning Helps Your Ecommerce Business. *Digital*. Online. https://digital.com/best-ecommerce-platforms/how-product-positioning-helps-your-ecommerce-business/.

Eilers, Christian. (2019). Glossary: 33+ Entrepreneurship Vocabulary Terms Defined. *Goodwall Blog*. https://www.goodwall.io/blog/entrepreneur-glossary/#

Enright, Mike. (2021). How to Overcome these Top 5 Small Business Fears and Challenges. *WoltersKluwer*. Online. 1st February 2021. https://www.wolterskluwer.com/en/expert-insights/how-to-overcome-these-top-5-small-business-fears-and-challenges.

Entrepreneur. (2015). Expert Advice: 10 Tips to Craft a Strong Business Plan. *Entrepreneur*. Online. https://www.entrepreneur.com/starting-a-business/expert-advice-10-tips-to-craft-a-strong-business-plan/241079.

EWOR Team. (2022). Are All Entrepreneurs Extremely Rich? *EWOR Team*. Online. 27th October 2022. https://ewor.io/are-all-entrepreneurs-extremely-rich/.

Failory. (2022) 16 Reasons Why 90% of eCommerces Fail. https://www.failory.com/blog/ecommerce-failure#

Farmiloe, Brett. (2023). Learning From Women-Owned Small Businesses: 12 Challenges & How to Overcome Them. *Score*. Online. 25th January 2023. https://www.score.org/resource/blog-post/learning-women-owned-small-businesses-12-challenges-how-over come-them

FatJoe. (2023). What are Backlinks? How to Get Them in 2021. *FatJoe*. Online. https://fatjoe.com/what-are-backlinks/?gclid=

Ferreira, Nicole Martins. (2020). How to Use Google Trends. 10 Mind-BlowingTricks for Entrepreneurs. https://www.oberlo.com/blog/google-trends.

Ferreira, Corey. (2022). What is Dropshipping and How Does it Work? (2023). *Shopify*. Online. 19th October 2022. https://www.shopify.com/uk/blog/what-is-dropshipping.

Forbes. (n.d). Jeff Bezos Profile. Online. https://www.forbes.com/profile/jeff-bezos/?sh=74c5f5ae1b23.

Forbes. (n.d). Oprah Winfrey Profile. Online. https://www.forbes.com/profile/oprah-winfrey/?sh=62895025745f

Forsey, Caroline. (2022). What is a Blog, and Why Should You Create One. *HubSpot.* Online. 16th September 2022. https://blog.hubspot.com/marketing/what-is-a-blog.

Freshbooks. (2020). 12 Real-World Pricing Strategy Examples. *Freshbooks.* Online. https://www.freshbooks.com/hub/leadership/12-real-world-pricing-strategy-examples

Gabrielle, Natasha. (2021). 1 in 3 Americans Have a Side Hustle. Here Are the Benefits to Having One. *NASDAQ.* July 24th 2021. Online. https://www.nasdaq.com/articles/1-in-3-americans-have-a-side-hustle.-here-are-the-benefits-to-having-one-2021-07-24.

Ganttpro. (2023). Marketing Action Plan Template. *Ganttpro.* Online. https://ganttpro.com/marketing-action-plan-template/

Gavril, Alexandra. (2017). A beginner's guide to writing title tags and meta descriptions that get clicks. *123 Reg Blog.* Online. https://www.123-reg.co.uk/blog/seo-2/a-beginners-guide-to-writing-title-tags-and-meta-descriptions-that-get-clicks/#

Gil, Gonzalo. (2021). How to write a business plan for your online business. *Shift 4 Shop.* Online. https://blog.shift4shop.com/how-to-write-a-business-plan.

Hancock, Gareth. (2022). Unique Selling Proposition Examples: 21 Brands That Get USP Right. *CXL.* Online. https://cxl.com/blog/unique-selling-proposition-examples/.

Hart, Meredith. (2023). What is a Niche Market? Examples, Benefits & How to Find One.

Hart, Meredith. (2022). 12 Examples of Positioning Statements & How to Craft Your Own. *HubSpot.* Online. https://blog.hubspot.com/sales/positioning-statement.

Heaslip, Emily. (2023). 7 Smart Pricing Strategies to Attract Customers. *CO.* Online. https://www.uschamber.com/co/run/finance/pricing-strategies-for-your-business

Heijmans, Michiel. (2020). Positioning your store in the online market. *Yoast.* Online. https://yoast.com/positioning-your-store-online/.

Heitman, Stephanie. (2022). How to Create the Most Effective Small Business Marketing Plan Ever (with a Template). *LocaliQ.* Online. https://localiq.com/blog/how-to-create-a-small-business-marketing-plan/.

Hines, Kristi. (2022). How to Write a Business Plan in 2023: The Ultimate Guide for Every Entrepreneur. *Oberlo.* Online. https://www.oberlo.com/blog/how-to-write-a-business-plan.

Hippos to Horses. (2021). How to Differentiate Your Online Business by Crafting a Point of Difference and a Reason to Believe (Even if you are Just Starting off) Online. https://www.hippostohorses.com/brand-positioning-statement-and-its-importance/.

Houraghan, Stephen. (2018). Brand Archetypes: The Definitive Guide [36 Examples]. *Iconic Fox.* Online. https://iconicfox.com.au/brand-archetypes/.

Howes, Dustin. (2021). How to grow your small business with affiliate marketing. *Zapier*. Online. https://zapier.com/blog/affiliate-marketing-for-small-business/.

Indeed. (n.d.). Examples of Niche Marketing for Small Business. Online. https://www. indeed.com/hire/c/info/niche-marketing

Ismail, Kayal. (2018). eBooks vs. Whitepapers: Which Performs Best? *CMSWire*. Online. 27th September 2018. https://www.cmswire.com/content-marketing/ebooks-vs-whitepa pers-which-performs-best/.

Jaskiewicz, Peter and James Combs. (2017). Nature versus nurture: Is an entrepreneur born or raised? *Financial Post*. Online. https://financialpost.com/entrepreneur/nature-versus-nurture-is-an-entrepreneur-born-or-raised.

Jobs, Steve. (n.d.) All about Steve Jobs. Online. https://allaboutstevejobs.com/verbatim/quotes

Jovancic, Nemanja. (2018). 58 Branding Quotes to Help Transform Your Brand Image. *LeadQuizzes*. Online. https://www.leadquizzes.com/blog/branding-quotes/.

Junttila, Henri. (n.d). How to Find a Profitable Niche for Your Online Business. *Lifehack*. Online. https://www.lifehack.org/articles/work/find-a-profitable-niche-online-busi ness.html.

Kamb, Steve. (2023). Welcome the Nerd Fitness Rebellion. *Nerd Fitness*. Online. https:// www.nerdfitness.com/about-2/#

Keenan, Michael. (2022). 12 Proven Marketing Strategies to Try (+ Examples and Tips). *Shopify*. Online. https://www.shopify.com/blog/marketing-strategies.

Kim, Grace. (2022). The Importance of an Effective Marketing Strategy in Reaching Your Business Goals. *Entrepreneur*. Online. April 22nd 2022. https://www.entrepreneur. com/growing-a-business/the-importance-of-an-effective-marketing-strategy-in/422521.

Law, Thomas J. (2022). Entrepreneurial Mindset. Online. https://www.oberlo.com/blog/ entrepreneurial-mindset

Lawrence, Sarah. (2020). How SoulCycle Lost Its Soul. Vox. Online. https://www.vox.com/ the-goods/22195549/soulcycle-decline-reopening-bullying-bike-explained

Lehmann, Sascha et al. (2020). The future of brand strategy: It's time to 'go electric.' *McKinsey*. Online. https://www.mckinsey.com/capabilities/growth-marketing-and-sales/ our-insights/the-future-of-brand-strategy-its-time-to-go-electric.

Levy, Steven. (n.d). Steve Jobs. *Encyclopaedia Britannica*. Online. https://www.britannica. com/biography/Steve-Jobs/Saving-Apple

Llao, Jillian. (2023). How to Create a Sales Plan in 10 Stept (+Free Template). *Fit Small Business*. Online. 89th March 2023. https://fitsmallbusiness.com/sales-plan-template/.

Louise. (2022). 4 Essential Elements to Building a Solid Brand Strategy. *Fleurir Online.* https://fleurironline.com/4-essential-elements-to-a-solid-brand-strategy/.

Mailchimp. (2022). How to Price Your Products to Turn a Profit. https://mailchimp.com/en-ca/resources/how-to-price-your-products-to-turn-a-profit/

Mailchimp. (2022). Branding Your Online Business. *Mailchimp.* Online. https://mailchimp.com/en-ca/resources/what-is-branding/

Mailchimp. (2022). How to Drive Repeat E-commerce Sales and Build Customer Loyalty. *Mailchimp.* Online. https://mailchimp.com/en-ca/resources/how-to-get-repeat-e-commerce-sales/.

Mandel, Janice. (2023). The Secret Ingredients in Georgetown Cupcakes. *StartupGrind.* Online. https://www.startupgrind.com/blog/the-secret-ingredients-in-georgetown-cupcake/.

MasterClass. (2021). Business 101: How to Develop an Entrepreneurial Mindset. https://www.masterclass.com/articles/how-to-develop-an-entrepreneurial-mindset

Matthew. (2022). Why Are Brand Values So Important (And How to Define Them)? *The Branding Journal.* Online. https://www.thebrandingjournal.com/2022/06/brand-values/#

McCormick, Kristen. (2020). 15+ Marketing Strategies for Small Businesses Worth Your Time & Money. *LocaliQ.* Online. https://localiq.com/blog/marketing-strategies-for-small-businesses/.

McDevitt, Haley. (2022). 7 Smart Marketing Strategies for Small Businesses. *Marketing Insider Group.* Online. https://marketinginsidergroup.com/marketing-strategy/small-business-marketing-strategies/.

Michael, Jonathan. (2023). 8 Quotes to Motivate You to Make a Plan and Stick to It. *BPlans.* Online. https://articles.bplans.com/8-quotes-to-motivate-you-to-make-a-plan-and-stick-to-it/.

Mind Tools Content Team. (n.d.) Perceptual Mapping. Online. https://www.mindtools.com/a1iixrj/perceptual-mapping

Morgaine, Briana. (n.d). What Do Successful Entrepreneurs Do in Their Off Time? *B Plans.* Online. https://articles.bplans.com/10-unlikely-hobbies-that-led-these-entrepreneurs-to-success/.

MotionPoint. (n.d.). What is Website Localization? *MotionPoint.* Online. https://www.motionpoint.com/translation/what-is-website-localization/

Murphy, Molly. (2021). 12 Examples of Positioning Statements and How to Write Your Own. *Sales Strategy.* Online. https://www.zendesk.co.uk/blog/positioning-statement-examples/#georedirect.

My Free Marketing. (2022). How Gary Vee Makes +$200,000,000/Year from 12 Businesses. Online. https://okdork.com/gary-vee-net-worth/

Nachlis, Jay. (2020). Start With the Customer and Work Backwards. *Coleman Insights*. Online. February 4th 2020. https://colemaninsights.com/coleman-insights-blog/start-with-the-customer-and-work-backwards#

Nethercott, Rustin. (2023). 5 of the Best Marketing Strategies You Haven't Tried Yet. *Constant Contact*. Online. https://www.constantcontact.com/blog/best-marketing-strategies/.

Nevogt, Dave. (2022). How to Develop an Entrepreneurial Mindset. *HubStaff*. Online. https://blog.hubstaff.com/entrepreneurial-mindset/.

Nexcess. (2022). 8 Steps to Write a Successful Online Store Business Plan. *Nexcess*. Online. https://www.nexcess.net/blog/online-store-business-plan/.

NFTE. (n.d.). Entrepreneurial Mindset. *NFTE*. Online. https://www.nfte.com/entrepreneurial-mindset/

Novak, Janette. (2019). How to Find a Niche Market in 4 Simple Steps. *Fit Small Business*. Online. https://fitsmallbusiness.com/how-to-find-niche-market/.

NWIBIZHUB. (n.d.). Develop an Entrepreneurial Mindset. NWIBIZHUB. Online. https://nwibizhub.com/develop-an-entrepreneurial-mindset/

Oberlo. (n.d.) How to use online search trends to identify business opportunities. Online. https://www.oberlo.com/blog/google-trends.

Ocasio, Kevin. (2023). SWOT Analysis Guide [Examples and FREE Template]. *Small Business Trends*. Online. https://smallbiztrends.com/2023/01/swot-analysis.html#google vignette.

Odjick, Desirae. (2022). How to Price a Product in 3 Simple Steps (2023). *Shopify*. Online. https://www.shopify.com/blog/how-to-price-your-product.

Odjick, Desirae. (2022). How To Write the Perfect Business Plan in 9 Steps (2023). *Shopify*. Online. https://www.shopify.com/blog/business-plan.

Ondreicsik, Ana. (n.d.) Perceptual Mapping. Conceptboard. Online. https://conceptboard.com/blog/perceptual-map-template/

One.com. (2023). What is Affiliate Marketing? *One.com*. Online. https://www.one.com/en/online-marketing/what-is-affiliate-marketing?

Patel, Neil. (n.d). What a Unique Selling Proposition Means & Why Your Businesses MUST Have One. Blog. https://neilpatel.com/blog/unique-selling-proposition/.

Perell, Kim. (2020). 5 Ways to Cultivate an Entrepreneurial Mindset. *Entrepreneur*. https://www.entrepreneur.com/leadership/5-ways-to-cultivate-an-entrepreneurial-mindset/357163.

Pofeldt, Elaine. (2019). Despite a Booming Job Market, Many Solopreneurs Opt to Stay Independent. Online. *Forbes*. https://www.forbes.com/sites/elainepofeldt/2019/06/22/despite-a-booming-job-market-many-solopreneurs-opt-to-stay-independent/?sh=48cec2381bb6.

Pompa, Matt. (2023). 30 Inspirational Entrepreneurs Quotes to Motivate Them for Greatness. *BigCommerce*. Online. https://www.bigcommerce.com/blog/quotes-for-entrepreneurs/.

QuickBooks. (2017). Overcoming 5 top challenges of international expansion. *QuickBooks Blog*. 19th May 2017. Online. https://quickbooks.intuit.com/r/growing-a-business/overcoming-5-top-challenges-of-international-expansion/.

Rampton, John. (2017). A 5-Step Formula to Find Your Niche. *ForbesTech*. Online. https://www.forbes.com/sites/johnrampton/2017/11/07/a-5-step-formula-to-find-your-niche/?sh=2506dbde48fc

Reddit. (n.d). Why Did You Decide to Start Your Own Business? Online. https://www.reddit.com/r/smallbusiness/comments/44vkou/why_did_you_decide_to_start_your_own_business/

Redpath Creative. (2019). A bucket of water and a sponge. Online. https://www.redpathcreative.co.uk/blog/2019/3/14/from-fork-lift-to-lift-off

Rock Content Writer. (2020). 6 Online Marketing Strategies for Small Businesses. *RockContent*. Online. https://rockcontent.com/blog/online-marketing-for-small-business/.

SBA. (n.d.). Market Research and Competitive Analysis. Online. https://www.sba.gov/business-guide/plan-your-business/market-research-competitive-analysis

Sheehan, Alexandra. (n.d.). What Is a Niche Market? 9 Examples + Products to Sell (2023). Online. https://www.shopify.com/blog/niche-markets.

Shewan, Dan. (2014). How to Write a Ferociously Unique Selling Proposition. *Marketing Ideas*. Online. https://www.wordstream.com/blog/ws/2014/04/07/unique-selling-proposition.

Small Business Administration. (n.d.). Marketing and Sales. *U.S Small Business Administration*. Online. https://www.sba.gov/business-guide/manage-your-business/marketing-sales.

Spark and Bloom Studio. (2021). Full Brand Strategy: Foundations, Positioning, Ideal Client, Personality, Messaging. *Spark and Bloom*. Online. https://sparkandbloomstudio.com/brand-strategy-case-studies.

Sridharan, Mithun. (2023). BLUF- How to Communicate Effectively and Persuasively? *Think Insights*. Online. https://thinkinsights.net/consulting/bluf/.

Startups. (2021). Entrepreneur Story: The Journey of Starting a Business. Online. https://fullscale.io/blog/entrepreneur-story-the-journey-of-starting-a-business/

Statista. (2022). Retail e-commerce sales worldwide from 2014 to 2026. Online. https://www.statista.com/statistics/379046/worldwide-retail-e-commerce-sales/

Systeme. (n.d.). Online Business Continues to Evolve: Here's How to Survive. Online. https://systeme.io/blog/online-business-evolve.

Tanner Accountants and Advisors. (2020). Shannon Klingman and Jennifer Gibson, Lume Deodorant. *Tanner.* Online. https://tannerco.com/shannon-klingman-and-jennifer-gibson-lume-deodorant/#

The Hartford. (2023). The 12 Brand Archetypes. Business Owner's Playbook. *The Hartford.* Online. https://www.thehartford.com/business-insurance/strategy/brand-archetypes/choosing-brand-archetype.

Thomsen, Rikke Berg. (2022). Man Crates Marketing: How to Turn $1,000 into $10+Million (Case Study). *Drip.com.* Online. https://www.drip.com/blog/man-crates-marketing.

ThriveThemes. (n.d.). Start an Online Business: Find Your Niche. Online. https://thrivethemes.com/start-online-business/find-your-niche/

Tikkanen, Amy. (n.d.) Oprah Winfrey. Encyclopaedia Britannica. Online. https://www.britannica.com/biography/Oprah-Winfrey

Todorov, Georgi. (2022) 110 Important Online Business Stats. Online. https://thrivemyway.com/online-business-stats/

Trackdeskblog. (2022). Strengthen Your Brand Identity through Affiliate Marketing. Online. 12th June 2022. https://trackdesk.com/blog/strengthen-your-brand-identity-through-affiliate-marketing.

Turbureanu, Liana. (2023). The Top 5 Benefits of Video Marketing in 2023. *Videowise.* Online. https://videowise.com/blog/the-top-5-benefits-of-video-marketing.

Twin, Alexandra. (2022). The 4 Ps of Marketing and How to Use Them in Your Strategy. *Investopedia.* Online. 14th December 2022. https://www.investopedia.com/terms/f/four-ps.asp.

US Small Business Administration. (n.d.) Write your business plan. *US Small Business Administration.* Online. https://www.sba.gov/business-guide/plan-your-business/write-your-business-plan.

Uzialko, Adam. (2023). Local Marketing Strategies for Success. *Business News Daily.* Online. https://www.businessnewsdaily.com/15770-local-marketing-strategies-for-small-business.html.

Vaynerchuk, Gary. Wikipedia. Online. https://en.wikipedia.org/wiki/Gary_Vaynerchuk

Vaynerchuk, Gary. Gary Vaynerchuk. Online. https://garyvaynerchuk.com/.

Vrountas, Ted. (2023). What is user-generated content, and how you should use it. *Instapage*. Online. https://instapage.com/blog/what-is-user-generated-content#

VWO. (2023). Website Optimization. *VWO*. Online. https://vwo.com/website-optimization/

Wahbe, Andrea. (2023). How to write a business plan in 10 steps + free template/ *Quick Books Blog*. Online. https://quickbooks.intuit.com/r/starting-a-business/business-plan-template/.

Wood, Meredith. (2021). The Beginner's Guide to Online Marketing for Small Business. *Fundera*. Online. https://www.fundera.com/blog/online-marketing-for-small-business.

Wooll, Maggie. (2022). 10 tips to find your niche and succeed at it. *Betterup*. https://www.betterup.com/blog/how-to-find-your-niche

Yu, Eric. (2022). 6 Must Read Pricing Strategy Quotes. *ProfitWell*. Online. https://www.priceintelligently.com/blog/bid/182007/6-must-read-pricing-strategy-quotes

Printed in Great Britain
by Amazon

45421735R00106